Palindromes
and
Anagrams

BY

HOWARD W. BERGERSON

Dover Publications, Inc.

New York

Published in Canada by General Publishing
Company, Ltd., 30 Lesmill Road, Don Mills,
Toronto, Ontario.
Published in the United Kingdom by Constable
and Company, Ltd., 10 Orange Street, London WC 2.

Palindromes and Anagrams is a new work, first
published by Dover Publications, Inc., in 1973.

International Standard Book Number: 0-486-20664-5
Library of Congress Catalog Card Number: 72-93286

Manufactured in the United States of America
Dover Publications, Inc.
180 Varick Street
New York, N. Y. 10014

INTRODUCTION

Palindromes and anagrams are subjects of great antiquity. It would be interesting to know something about the vagaries of their literary status over the millennia, but, so far as I know, there exists no book which adequately reviews these subjects against the great background of history. The historical information I have received from the aficionados has consisted mostly of tantalizing bits and pieces, and although some source items have been comparatively substantial, even these would do little more than whet the appetite of the confirmed logophile who yearns for a definitive work. For example, George Marvill, of Leeds, Yorkshire, picked up William Dobson's *Poetical Ingenuities* (published in England in 1882) at a second-hand stall, and after imbibing it for a number of years until he had it by heart, lent it to me. In it a fascinating account of anagrams is given. One may read, for example, that in the seventeenth century anagrams were the literary passion of the day.

Palindromes seem to have been less written about than anagrams by the old authors, and so it is more difficult in the case of palindromes to be certain that they have always been important enough to rate their own muse. But, whether those strange individuals so inexplicably obsessed with reversible writing have always been with us or not, it would at least seem safe to say that no official post has ever been created specifically for a palindromist. Such, however, is not the case where anagrams are concerned. In France, Louis XIII appointed Thomas Billon to be his Royal Anagrammatist. Any ruler who will so honor even one such Alchemist of Words can't be all bad. We, the currently quick, however, tend to regard both palindromes and anagrams as mere curiosa. It is noteworthy that serious essays bearing such ponderous titles as "The Political Responsibilities of the Poet" occasion us no surprise, because poetry is an art; but a title such as "The Political Responsibilities of the Palindromist" would strike us as risible. Behind this lurks the entrenched thought that the palindrome (ditto the anagram) is not Art.

Nevertheless, these rococo oddments are not really separated from the "mainstream" of "normal" writing by any unbridgeable gap, for it is entirely possible to accomplish the transition from (for example) palindromic to nonpalindromic writing in a fairly smooth, reasonably continuous way. To gain an inkling of how such a transition might be made, consider, firstly, palindromes of the letter-unit variety—those which read backward just as they do forward, letter by letter, and with which we are chiefly concerned. A preeminent example of such a palindrome in English is the following universally admired gem—mined, cut, and polished by Leigh Mercer, of London:

A man, a plan, a canal—Panama

of which Alastair Reid has written (though he mistakenly attributed it to James Thurber, in his book *Passwords**) that "it deserves to be enshrined on a monument, since, besides fulfilling its difficult technical requirements, it rings with true acclaim"; which David L. Silverman, of Beverly Hills, has called "the ultimate in palindromic engineering"; and which J. A. Lindon, of Weybridge, Surrey, has done the honor of palindromically parodying:

A dog, a pant, a panic in a Patna pagoda.

It would be possible, however, to choose units larger than single letters, such as digrams (pairs of consecutive letters), for example, or trigrams; or, alternately, units of entirely different kinds, having variable length, such as syllables, morphemes, or words. From the work of J. A. Lindon—author of many an intriguing word-unit palindrome—I pluck this example:

LOVE IS THIS AND THIS IS LOVE

Darling, my love
Is great, so great;
Recalling Heaven's calm above.

---

* Atlantic–Little, Brown and Co., 1959.

Fate is sweet this—
All after Fall!
Fall? After all,
This, sweet, is fate—
Above calm Heaven's recalling.

Great, so great is
Love, my darling!

There can be palindromes in which phrases are the units, or in which sentences, or lines of poetry, are the units, and still others in which the units are paragraphs or stanzas. It is only when the mathematical limit is reached—when the whole poem, story, essay, or laundry list is taken as the unit—that the palindromicness, having been increasingly attenuated at each successive step, at last completely vanishes. But all the countless things that dwell in the misty mid-region short of that limit, such as "The Highwayman," by Alfred Noyes, with its opening stanzas approximately repeated at the end, still retain some slight tinge of palindromicity. Similar remarks apply to anagrams. (In particular, the chapter on vocabularyclept poetry deals actually with word-unit anagrams.)

So much for the "vertical" dimension along which palindromes and anagrams pass imperceptibly into ordinary no-nonsense poetry and workaday prose. Now—before passing on to other matters—let us take a fleeting glance at the "horizontal" dimension, through which the affiliations of palindromes and anagrams with other forms of "verbal ingenuities" can be traced. For readers unacquainted with anagrams, a superb example provided by George Marvill will serve to illustrate what an anagram is: the re-arranging of the letters of a given word, name, phrase, sentence, or other expression to form another, often (but not necessarily) apposite, expression. This anagram was composed by Timothy Shy (D. B. Wyndham Lewis) of the now defunct London *News-Chronicle*, on the repeal of the Eighteenth Amendment during F. D. Roosevelt's first Presidential term:

Franklin Delano Roosevelt.   Tons o' drink, even ale, for all.

A palindrome having an even number of letters is, clearly, also a species of anagram, since its last half uses the same letters as its first half (as in "Kay, a red nude, peeped under a yak"—J. A. Lindon), though the order of the letters is not scrambled, but simply reversed. A palindrome with an odd number of letters is excluded from the class of anagrams only by the presence of the center letter (as in "'Miry rim! So many daffodils,' Delia wailed, 'slid off a dynamo's miry rim!'"—J. A. Lindon).

Charades—in the sense in which the word is used in this book— are too a species of anagram, for, again, the two parts of a charade make use of the same letters, just as in anagrams, though in charades the order of the letters is left entirely unaltered:

> Amiable together.
> Am I able to get her?

Palindromes and charades are not necessarily mutually exclusive of each other, either, as may be seen from the fact that the charade below contains within itself the palindrome, "Flee to me, remote elf":

> How fleet, O mere mote elfin, ever lovely in groves.
> How flee to me, remote elf? I never love lying roves.

Anagrams may also be pangrams (short compositions—sentences, lines of poetry, etc.—which use every letter of the alphabet). In the verse below, concocted by Edwin Fitzpatrick, a nineteenth-century logologist and logological poet—a figure so legendary some say he may never have existed at all—the lines are all pangrammatic as well as all mutually anagrammatic. Each line contains each of the twenty consonants once, and each of the six vowels (a, e, i, o, u, y) twice:

> Why jog exquisite bulk, fond crazy vamp,
> Daft buxom jonquil, zephyr's gawky vice?
> Guy fed by work, quiz Jove's xanthic lamp—
> Zow! Qualms by déjà vu gyp fox-kin thrice.

Palindromes may also be lipograms (compositions which exclude by fiat certain letters of the alphabet). A palindrome will usually exclude some letters of the alphabet out of necessity, so that in order to be considered a lipogram it will need to exclude even more letters. The most elegant and entertaining example of a lipogrammatical palindrome—one using only four letters of the alphabet—that I have seen, was composed by George Marvill, and first appeared in the *New Statesman* (Weekend Competition), May 5, 1967:

PALINDROMIC CONVERSATION BETWEEN TWO OWLS

> "Too hot to hoot!"
> "Too hot to woo!"
> "Too wot?"
> "Too hot to hoot!"
> "To woo!"
> "Too wot?"
> "To hoot! Too hot to hoot!"

Looking to the other extreme, an example of a pangrammatic palindrome can be found in the works of the strange Edwin Fitzpatrick. It will be noted, however, that Fitzpatrick's palindromic pangram sorely lacks the lucidity which graces the palindromic and lipogrammatic Owls above:

> Oh, wet Alex—a jar, a fag!
> Up, disk, curve by!
> Man Oz, Iraq, Arizona, my Bev?
> Ruck's id-pug—a far Ajax—elate?
> Who?

Of course, "normal palindromic writing" often is—or at least ought to be—comparatively free of the impenetrable obscurity that bedevils the above "oddity." Take, as a case in point, this superb example of *reversibl—vers libre* (to speak anagrammatically) by the English poet, Alastair Reid:

> T. Eliot, top bard,
> Notes putrid tang emanating, is sad.
> I'd assign it a name:
> "Gnat dirt upset on drab pot toilet."

It must be admitted, however, that most palindromic poets, past and present, have scrutinized the virtue of clarity through low-priority spectacles. Clarity is really only one of a number of desiderata, which, taken all together, may be called "The integrity of the dream," for poetry is dreaming, and palindromic poetry in particular is letter-symmetrical dreaming. The palindromic poet's only obligation is that his palindromic dream should have a clear meaning for *him*; for, obviously, the reader—if he finds the poem obscure—has a right to the assurance that there exists a meaning to be discovered. To the extent that the palindromic poet meets this obligation—and granting also that his dreams are sufficiently interesting—his work will inevitably achieve the exalted status of "exposition fodder" for the students and critics of his time.

It was said that students, coming to the shadowy Fitzpatrick for clarification of his poem "Elegy on the Death of Sister Nita and Her Cat, Bigot,"* would be told a strange story of seven sisters that he knew—Adine, Naomi, Sibyl, Amoret, Nola, Enid, and Debra (an eighth sister, Nita, was shunned because she was shaped like an urn)—until the students would flee from the interview in confusion. Perhaps the story of the sisters was one Fitzpatrick dreamed (since urn-shaped people do not abound in medical records, and would seem to be rather useful if they did); it is no contradiction because the fact is that dreams *are* truths, and, what is more, every palindromic poem, like every work of art, is the expression of a dream. The interested reader may read Fitzgerald's "Elegy" and decide for himself. A briefer illustration of how palindromic necessity and the dreaming mind interact will be suitable here.

Imagine a great violinist playing sacred music to a rapt audience. Suddenly, fibrous fruits begin to grow with fantastic rapidity, unseen, within the body of the violin, debasing its tone to a mangled squawk, murdering the music, and destroying the virtuoso's reputation, as well as his whole life, all in a few seconds:

> Loofahs in a violin!
> In a gap in my hymn, I—Paganini!—lo, I vanish,
> A fool!

Obviously, this could happen only in a dream.

The subject of anagrams extends practically to infinity. Medieval wordmen could no doubt tell us of various clever games, anagrammatical and otherwise, that monkish people worked out. Nowadays the more erudite crossword puzzles are the home of innumerable subtle anagrams. Anagrams may even provide interesting techniques for generating poetry. For example, suppose a first line to be freely written. The second line must then be an anagram of the first. The third line is again free, and so on. The theory is that the poet who writes in this form, due to the fact that when he writes a free line, he creates anagrammatical constraints for himself which will have an unpredictable influence on the next line, will inevitably invent poetry

---

* See page 17.

of a kind that he could not otherwise imagine. Once upon a time a romantic schoolgirl set pen to paper and, after careful thought, wrote as follows:

Now and then we met in dreamy rainbow bowers.

In the effort of anagramming, she found her modest talent considerably amplified, and the second line proved quite an improvement over the first:

Bonny hand at window—we twain remember Rose.

This, then, gave her the idea for her free third line—which, consequently, took a totally unforeseen direction ("Her violets and cowslips had been her favorite flowers"). Ultimately, many hours and anagrams later, she ended it thus:

Wand wetted in elfish ethers, pickled in froth for two,
And sprinkled with the confetti of withered flowers.

As a sidelight, one may wonder what would happen if television (where the letters can be moved around on the screen) ever became conscious of the application of anagrams to advertising. Recently, my son, Earl (age twelve), discovered this remarkable transformation: HEY, DOG! RUN!—GREYHOUND. Madison Avenue, take note.

Readers who are interested in reading further about anagrams, palindromes, and related linguistic recreations may wish to subscribe to *Word Ways*, a magazine published four times a year since 1968 (A. Ross Eckler, Spring Valley Road, Morristown, New Jersey 07960). Those who are more interested in solving word-puzzles including anagrams, rebuses, charades, and the like, in friendly competition with others, can join the National Puzzlers' League, which publishes a monthly newsletter, *The Enigma* (Paul E. Thompson, E. Alstead Road, Alstead, New Hampshire 03602).

I wish to thank Leigh Mercer, Dr. A. Ross Eckler, Erik Bodin, William G. Bryan, Alastair Reid (of Fife, Scotland), Graham Reynolds, John Wardroper (both of London), Darryl Francis (of Hounslow, Middlesex, England), John McClellan, Dmitri Borgmann, Yuen Ren Chao, George Marvill, and J. A. Lindon for their contributions to this volume; and, lastly, I can only say that it is beyond my poor power to calculate how much the existence of this book owes to the help and encouragement of my wife, *Nellie Bergerson*, an MS victim, who is, without a doubt (anagrammatically speaking), a *serene, noble girl*.

CONTENTS

Nothing is so characteristic of the artist as his power of shaping his work, of subjugating his raw material, however aberrant it be from what we call normality, to the consistency of nature.

–Lionel Trilling, The Liberal Imagination

Palindromes and Charades

or Literary Chess

A palindrome is a word, verse, or sentence that is the same when read backward or forward, letter by letter. Palindromic poems and their composition are a subject with a long history. The inventor of palindromic verse, so it is alleged, was one Sotades of Maroneia (in Thrace), a Greek poet and satirist of the third century B.C. The story goes that he made the mistake of lampooning Ptolemy II Philadelphus, who had him captured, sealed in a lead box, and cast into the ocean.

A high-water mark in the history of palindromic poetry was the publication in 1802 of a 416-line poem, "Ethopoiia Karkinike," by Ambrose Hieromonachus Pamperes, a modern Greek who composed the poem in ancient Greek. This poem is composed of 416 short (line-length) palindromes.

J. A. Lindon, writing in the November, 1966, *Worm Runner's Digest*, had this to say about the composition of such comparatively short palindromes:

> It takes two to make a game of chess, the other being of course the Adversary. Black may well resolve beforehand to play the Caro-Kann or King's Indian, on which he is an expert, but soon, with a scattering of White pawns, a knight and a bishop at his elbow, he finds himself, willy-nilly, embroiled in the complexities of the Three Sailors' Gambit.
>
> The palindromist is in a similar case, for here too the Devil takes a hand. As many impish malignities wad out the pages of the dictionary as ever diabolised within Bill Snyth's crystal. In vain the palindromist may decide that his next effort shall be a perfectly constructed sentence, containing nothing but what is apt; for every word he uses must also be used in reverse, and it is here that irrelevancies creep in. In real life a cigar is not necessarily tragic, nor do dairymen arrive in myriads. In Palindromia, however—

What is true of palindromic sentences is true many times over for full-length poems which are end-to-end palindromes. Consequently, the possibility of composing such palindromic poems has almost never been taken seriously. It has been understandably supposed that no really worthwhile literary creation can be made in this way. But this is perhaps a matter of values. One can with equal justice aver that the composing of palindromes is a fine art, at least as much as is chess. The palindromic poet's purpose is to try to make something new and different *via words as such*, letting their meanings go hang, relatively—at any rate their more familiar associations. Therefore I shall now make so bold as to declare, once and for all, that palindromes are literary chess. But because palindromes are (as will be seen) only half the story, I must hasten to add that they are only that half of literary chess in which the Devil plays the Whites.

Poetry is evocation. Chess, too, evokes its own species of wonder. Nicely combined as palindromes, poetry and chess should pulse with a hybrid élan unknown to either of them taken alone. We shall see if there is anything to this fanciful hypothesis. We shall also see how exceedingly busy the Devil has been, trying to keep the poet from bringing order out of chaos.

In the group of three palindromes presented below, the first is a minuscule drama in which Ida speaks the first six lines and Ben the last eight. The second is a more rhapsodic type of poem. The third is again a dramatic poem, though of slightly more ample proportions, which seems to exhibit at least the illusion of a plot, climax, sustained mood, and continuity of thought.

IDA BY THE WINDOW

Ma, I so resign.
It's all a poet air.
Ben is, I see, so Greek.
In sly dissent I wore no gay ruff.
O see by a brae his nag roll or yaw?
Awol laws (as are every god's) are a dire rod.

"Aye, fade with gin—O, too wispily,
Sordid rosy lips I woo.
(Tonight I wed a fey adorer, Ida.)
Eras do gyre—veer as a swallow away.

Roll, organs I hear! Bay, bees of fury ago!
Nero, witness idyls Nike ergo sees!
Is inebriate Opal lasting? Is Eros?
I am!"

THE FADED BLOOMERS' RHAPSODY

Flee to me, remote elf—Sal a dewan desired;
Now is a Late-Petal Era.
We fade: lucid Iris, red Rose of Sharon;
Goldenrod a silly ram ate.
Wan Olives teem (ah, Satan lives!);
A star eyes pale Roses.

Revel, big elf on a mayonnaise man—
A tinsel baton-dragging nice elf too.
Lisp, Oh Sibyl, dragging Nola along;
Niggardly bishops I loot.
Fleecing niggard notables Nita names,
I annoy a Man of Legible Verse.

So relapse, ye rats,
As evil Natasha meets Evil
On a wet, amaryllis-adorned log.
Norah's foes' orders (I ridiculed a few) are late, Pet.
Alas, I wonder! Is Edna wed?
Alas—flee to me, remote elf.

EDNA WATERFALL

Deliver no evil, avid diva I saw die.
Render an unsung aria for erotogenic id.
O never egg Alec Naif, fairer Edna Waterfall,
A nonassimilative, volatile reef-dweller—apparelless brag!
Natasha I saw die, render an unsung aria.
For Edna Waterfall—a liar—familiar feuds live:
Dastard Ogre and Edna!
Pupils, one tacit song or poem—or didos deft.
Celestial lives (Ida rapt as Naomi)
Laud smegma, alas—keep never a frondlet on.

So did no solo snoop malign
Irised sad eyen. Oh dewed yen—
Oh tressed May noon, hello! Tacit songs rev!
Love's barge of assent carts base tarts,
A cerise deb abed, unreined flesh.
Sin—a viand—Edna sees and Edna has,
Or bust fossettes, or redder rosettes.
Soft sub-rosa hand Edna sees,
And, Edna, I vanish—self-denier!
Nude babe, desire castrates abstractness.
A foe grabs Evolver's Gnostic Atoll, eh? No!
On, yam (dessert-honeydewed), honeyed as desiring!
I lampoon solos on didos. Not eld nor far
(Even peek! "Salaam, gems dual," I moan)
Sat Paradise Villa, its elect fed.
So did Romeo prognosticate no slip up,
And Edna, ergo, drats a devil's due:
"Frail! I'm a frail all a-fret, a-wander!
O fair Agnus nun, a red Nereid was I.
Ah Satan, garb's seller,
Apparel (lewd fee) relit a love vital I miss anon.
All a-fret, a wanderer I affiance—
Lagger even odic—in ego 'torero.'
Fair Agnus nun, a red Nereid was I.
Avid diva, live on reviled."

Charades are, as we have indicated in the Introduction, duplex compositions in which each of two parts utilize the same letters in the same order, but break the words at different points so as to produce different meanings. Charades are the obverse side of the coin of which palindromes are the reverse side. In charades, just as in palindromes, each new verbal brick added appears in two different forms, having two distinct meanings, both of which must fit. Though the difference is only barely perceptible, charades are slightly less difficult than palindromes. Therefore we may say that charades are literary chess in which the Devil plays the Blacks:

Hiss, caress pursuit, or astound, O roc—O cobras.
His scares spur suitor as to undo rococo bras.

Charades, unlike palindromes, have very little history behind them, and not much has been done with them. They need not be merely couplet length, as in the above example and all the other examples shown here, but, so far, no one has composed any longer ones. Charades and palindromes, in couplet length, dovetail nicely to yield the elegant stanza that Edwin Fitzpatrick (not to be confused with the more famous Edward Fitzgerald) used in his quite eccentric translation of Omar Khayyám, called "The Rubaiyat of Charades and Palindromes." Of the following palindromes and charades, those which are combined into quatrains rhyming A A B A are selected from Fitzpatrick's little-known opus. All the others—couplet length charades, couplet length palindromes (often combined to make rhyming quatrains), quatrain length palindromes (one of which is in rhyme), and longer palindromes—are from the fantasque oriental dancing song, "Fling Thong," from "O Tongue in Cheek." Many have never forgotten the debut of that opera, from its heavenly overture to its final love duet, "O Tongue in Cheek, Thy Name is Insincerity," a negative consummation so devoutly to be avoided that the opera was never given again. Although the curtain was rung down amid monstrous, cacophonic applause, no encores were asked for. Everybody filed out of the opera house in an agony of diminishment, with the hero's last and noblest sentiments still insulting their injured ears:

> No, nay! Nat is too bossy, as I say,
> "Go! Be off for a fat salami!"
> Aloof, at lovers I had named I stare.
> Here smegma is food, a kimono is secret sin.
> I misled a ticklish sultan at lush silk citadels I minister.
> Cession, O Mikado, of Siam Gems ere he rats, I demand!
> Ah—is revolt a fool aim?
> (A last, a far-off foe—bogy as I—says so.)
> Boots it any anon?

In contemplating such a semantically degenerate palindrome as this one, the reader can, I trust, feel in his very bones how closely the Devil has come to checkmating the opera's valiant, embattled librettist. After all, who would ever say, "Boots it any anon"?

I begin the dual-source quotations with a palindromic quatrain which is distinctly self-referential, since it refers to the art of the ill-fated Sotades. Fitzpatrick has been dead for many decades, so we need not worry about him, but it is to be hoped that the sainted librettist of "O Tongue in Cheek" (who is now very old) will not ultimately suffer a fate similar to that of Sotades of old. Such a thing might have been all right for Sotades, but for this old friend of a great composer to be captured, sealed in a lead box, and sunk to the bottom of the sea would be too ignoble an end. After all, *his* palindromes (and charades!) were once supported by a full symphonic orchestra, and not merely a zither. (Sticklers for accuracy will find here two small slips by the librettist; they were pointed out to him but he insisted on keeping them, saying that the mood of the poem required them.)

Selections from "Fling Thong" and from "The Rubaiyat of Charades and Palindromes"

Nora, by my llano,
I to mellific Ida toss drowsy astral-age roses.
Ava, put up a vase so regal.
(Art says words Sotadic I fill emotionally, my baron.)

To id: If I, an emoter, cannot fight or fall,
Or, frustrated, I bay and do sit—'tis odd.
Nay! Abide, tart surf! Roll a froth gift on nacre to me—
Naif idiot.

Eras bolster aback Cuba.
Eyes nettle forensic ire to sere drums, Sam—
Mass-murder esoteric is.
(Nero felt tense? Yea, buck cabaret slobs are!)

Rail at natal bosh, aloof gibbons!
   Snob-bird named "Red Rose of Mine Desire!"
Rise, denim foes! Order—demand ribbons,
   Snob—big fool! Ah, so blatant a liar!

Play carols on rebec, inspired osteopath. Gino,
Tonight a poet's ode rips Nice, Bern, Oslo, racy Alp.

Flamingo pale, scenting a latent shark
Flaming opalescent in gala tents—hark!

Red nowise, nor dynast, I—more venal—
Led tressed Anna Melba to pander.
Oh base id! Nudes abed (Iris and Ella) chose it!

In Melos on desserts I lived;
I merit tasseltops, rose calyxes,
Sexy laces or spotless attire.
Mid evil, I stressed no solemnities:
"Oh call Edna, Sir! I debased undies abhor!"
"Edna! Potable manna! Dessert!"
(Della never omits any drones? I wonder!)

No, uncle-and-auntless be, as ties deny our end.
No unclean, dauntless beasties den you rend.

Elapse, Time—relative gate to my agony.
By no gay motet age vital eremites pale.

"Torero, with cayenne I (Sir Apostle) fire volts—ah,
Hast lover?" . . . (I felt so Parisienne—yacht I wore . . . rot!)

O fly, rich Eros—dogtrot, ski, orbit eras put in swart
Of lyric heros. Dog Trotski or bite Rasputin's wart.

Natasha, Naomi, and Edna deflate men in rut.
A slob myself, I ratted never—
I dare hot drawers at uppity-bred salons.
I'd lose money, O doyen? O me! Sold is Nola's derby tip!
Put as reward to her a dire vendetta rifle,
Symbol saturnine, metal-fed—
And, Edna, I moan, "Ah Satan!"

Ah, Steppe-rim Edna whom Ida did abed instruct,
Sentinel Ivan is a moody ruffian.
I—gavel-banger—ponder a ban defied.
I cede no law, or rosy amorists err. A civic arrest, Sir!
O, may sorrow alone decide if Edna bared no pregnable vagina,
If fury doom as in a vile nit-nest Curt Snide!
Bad Ida (dim—Oh wan demirep!) pets? Ha!

Ramona is reposed under ruffles, as I and Edna;
And Edna is a self-furred nude so Persian, Omar.

Ya! No spy lacks urbanity! Gnaw, toot not
On too twangy tin a brusk calypso! Nay!

Egad, no boy abed unbuckled Ella!
Be ye bardic if in gambols, titan amative clod.
Altar flowers send. Lo, dip a staff!

O pass Anita nosegays, so manic in a motor;
Exalt fossettes or redder rosettes—
Soft, lax, erotomanic in a mossy age.
Sonatinas—sap of fat, sapid oldness—re-wolf, rat!
La dolce vita, man! At it, slob magnific!
I—drab-eyeballed elk cub (nude)—bay, "O bondage!"

Forgo thick ale. "I do's" cope softest—opaled, sob-lade;
For gothic kaleidoscopes oft estop aled-so blade.

Loop, dip, mild natal fay, by a water.
Fret away by a flat and limpid pool.

Ha! Thou tragedy ingrate, dwell on—superb old stag—in gloom.
Hath outrage, dying, rated well? On super-bold staging loom!
  Moody spigot dew, sag assured. Roar, zero-tide!
Editor Ezra, order us sagas wed to gipsy doom.

Forbear, Sandra, rest. Cry, stallion, or bray in gloom,
For bears and rarest crystal lion, orb raying, loom.
  Moo, lost elk—O orbs amid wonders awed. Was it a bat?
I saw dew as red, now dim as brooklet so loom.

How fleet, O mere mote elfin—ever lovely in groves.
How flee to me, remote elf? I never love lying roves.

Coo, lisp, or to a mate urban joyously come, Dian.
Cool, I sport. O amateur banjo, you sly comedian,
  No sail had dahlias on, tra la—Roman air, allude to Ned.
Denote, dull Arian, a moral art—no sail had dahlias on.

Flu galled an illiterate elf. Reed-sung maiden woos.
  So owned I am! (Gnus, deer, fleet are—till in a dell, a gulf.)
Flow, alas, solo cosmic. A lily motif use.
  Sufi, to my Lilac I'm so colossal a wolf.

Hiss, caress pursuit, or astound, O roc—O cobra.
His scares spur suitor as to undo rococo bra.
  A harem must nag eleemosynary tramps. A live
Evil asp martyr any some elegant summer? Aha!

Hips! and, allegro! Man cedes. I reach ego's tab.
Hip, sandal, leg, romance, desire, ache—go stab
  Barcarole's summer. Aha, royal penalties abed
Debase it—lane-play or a harem, mussel or a crab.

Barb a rainbow, ersatz one, soft a-booing age.
Barbara in bowers at zones of taboo ingage.
  Egad, loon Sahib, Barbara naps again—
I a-gasp! An Arab rabbi has no old age.

Spitfires sap Sir Cecil. A brevet alibis pillager.
  Regal lip, sibilate verbal ice crisp as serif tips.
Spill a germ or feral bit, Alcestis! O Pan, erase villager!
  "Regal lives' arena posits eclat!" I blare from regal lips.

Ana, crass, a mad nadir ate. Who meets Etna? I (dark coma!),
  A mock-radiant esteem (Oh wet-arid!), and a mass-arcana.
Anadem, Ah! Saturnism! O sob, nude baroness—Apostolate Roma.
  Amoret, a lot so passé! Nor abed unbosom sin—rut ashamed, Ana.

I saw Nerissa, pure in water—
Eve's mirror!
Edna, with gilded light I wander,
Or rim severe, tawnier upas;
Siren was I!

Tress astir, copy hedonism. O sob, nude baroness—elicit
  Tic I lessen, or a-bed unbosom sin-ode. Hypocrits assert
Truce, tone-volatile. We, my belle, can we help miss it?
  'Tis simple: hew nacelle by me. (We lit a love-note curt!)

Oft woman's laugh, terse as esthetic-offish, yowls
Of two manslaughters—eases the tic of fishy owls;
  Slew obstacled if nided rows at a Roman idol, Canis.
Sin, a clod-inamorata, sworded infidel cats' bowels.

Infant, as queen or mouse ye sin (estimably thereto, as Ted's will).
In fantasque enormous eyes I nest. I'm a blythe retoasted swill.
  Lid off a daffodil I doff adays (at scenic idol-embargos),
So grab (melodic in ecstasy) a daffodil. I doff a daffodil.

War bled Paris till a veranda birdie
Warbled. (Par I still aver, and a birdie.)
  "I'd revel—bong! Illicit song!" Aida signals.
(Slang is a diagnostic ill, ignoble Verdi.)

Emdee, her art so melts a chassé legato of
  Foot ageless. Ah, castle most rare, heed me.
Ye knave, negate snide Slavic ire to see us sign it "Love."
  Revolting issue! Esoteric, I valsed in—set a Genevan key.

Nostril flare for erotic ova, hag? Ah so.
  O shag a havoc! I (torero feral) flirt, son.
Now revolts Olympus, ogre volcano.
  On a clover go sup, my lost lover won.

Forsooth, Ingrid, dance. I sat alone late,
For soothing riddance is a talon elate.
  Etamine dragon, Nimrod rehems Eva's dimity.
My Timid saves me her dorm. In no garden I mate.

Spa élan aids racy Alpha-jar.
  Rajah, play cars. Diana leaps!
Speed, panel-bib Noel car! I'm on Devil Star!
  Rats lived no miracle on bible-nap deeps!

Without familiarity with the opera, many passages from "Fling Thong" could easily be given a completely erroneous interpretation. Skipping through the pages, one finds the characters saying, "Debase wedlock, cold ewes abed!" "Dog-deifiers reified God!" "On a tip, act, Capitano!" and "Stark rabid, I bark, 'Rats!'" or maybe "O desirable Melba, rise, do!" and "Cite operas as are poetic!" From the longer passages, the recitatives, the browsing eye can pluck such palindromically potent phrases as "O, jadedness ended a joy."

      Clan, galling us—to and fro, music and art
      Clang all in gusto, and from us I can dart.
        Trap-edified afore, wolfed is yawning Io-cave.
      Eva, coign-in-wayside flower, O fade if I depart.

      Diana, sit rapt! So melts a chassé legato of
        Foot ageless. Ah, castle most partisan, aid!
      Diary? No, miladi. Dross verbal by a grot, a cove?
      Evocator gay, blab revs sordid alimony raid.

      Nude, note not oceanic ace piano
        On a ipecac in a ecotone, tone dun.
      Nurse ye no yen, O melodic ace piano.
        On a ipecac I dole money. On eyes run . . .

      Malcontent eye, vile by a grot, a cove—
        Evocator gay, be—live, yet net no clam.
      Maiden, if no craft so melts a chassé legato of
        Foot ageless—Ah, castle most far, confined I am.

Moor, garb music sidereal—lived urban.
Nab rude villa ere disc is umbra, groom.
Mood-gal, spur a famine fatal. I attach turban.
Nab Ruth, cattail at a fen. I'm afar up slag-doom.

De-lifed Eros' halo dims. I won, foam-god.
Dogma-of-Nowism idol—ah, sore defiled,
Deliver won eras to grasp! Oh sibyl, laud!
Dually bishops' argots are now reviled.

Turrets yodel, baffled doe, to me. Remote elf
Flee to me. Remote odd elf—fabled oyster—rut.
Tulsa, Miami (and enrol Boston), odd as
Sad—do not sob. Lorn Edna I maim—a slut.

Fled as aye, fond light-rimmed aid,
Diadem-mirth, gild no fey (a sad elf).
Flow dolce, song of bard—nor after
Fret far on drab fog (nose-cold wolf).

Nonaloof as dew's part-paste, satin-new gems,
Pink lilac, I go.
Lo, my tetrad, abet a caviare poem.
Oh, as a torsade lucid, I revise it; I sob.
Revel, Bali Miss, a-nude. Tide is in.
O dare her, Adonis.
I edited unassimilable verbosities I've ridiculed as rot.
As a home opera I vacate,
Bad art (etymological ilk) nips me, Gwen.
Nita set sap-traps, weds a fool anon.

Elapse, song. Upset, at sea, I long. A melody, a meow—
Woe may dole magnolia estates pugnoses pale.
Elated is debased Oberon. So that solid, naive vow
Wove viand I lost! Ah, to snore bodes a bedside tale.

The Life and Death of Sydney Yendys

GEORGE MARVILL

Sydney Yendys was born, destined, preordained, doomed, to be a palindromist. His birth-year was 1881, an arrangement of figures which reads the same left to right, right to left, and upside down. He was christened Sydney, a reversal of the order of the letters of his surname. His first coherent utterance was "Dad-dad-dad-dad-dad-dad-dad-dad!" followed in due course by "Mam-mam-mam-mam-mam-mam-mam-mam!" Later in life he was to marry a girl called Edna, and to have a daughter, also named Edna. What more useful piece of equipment, in times of emergency, can a palindromist have than a pair of Ednas?

Fate didn't begin to show its hand until he had been a married man and a parent for some five years. Up to then he had led a blameless life as a bookkeeper with the OK Cartrac Ko. Business expanded until one day a junior bookkeeper named Wordrow was engaged to assist Sydney in his duties.

"I say," said Wordrow a week or two later, "ever noticed your name's a palindrome?"

"Eh?" said Sydney. "What's a palindrome?" He had never heard the word; or if he had, he had a vague idea it was some sort of low-down variety theatre.

"I was reading about 'em in the puzzle corner in my Sunday paper," said Wordrow. "It's a word, or a sentence, that reads the same forwards or backwards. Like—like, say, 'level,' or 'Rats live on no evil star.'"

Sydney wrote on his blotting paper the capital letters S-Y-D-N-E-Y Y-E-N-D-Y-S. "I say!" he cried. "You're right! They are! They're just the same backwards as forwards."

"Funny you've never noticed it before," said Wordrow. (He was never very bright.) "*I* should have spotted it right away."

Sydney said nothing. He sat staring spellbound at the combination of letters on his blotting-paper. Destiny had taken over.

From then on he became more and more obsessed by palindromes. As other men spend all their waking hours thinking of golf or chess, Sydney devoted all his spare time—and some of the time he should have spent in keeping the Cartrac books—in jotting down word-pairs like "lived-devil," "god-dog," "Dennis-sinned," and "flog-golf." Wordrow caught some of his enthusiasm, and the two would scribble palindromic sentences on scraps of paper and toss them across to each other. When Wordrow offered "K cab back," Sydney retorted "Wot? No smart trams on tow?" and when Wordrow came back with "'E finks it's old Otto'd lost 'is knife," Sydney's snappy catch-answer was "Paget saw an Irish tooth, sir, in a waste gap."

One day Sydney saw the results of a palindromic competition published in a weekly paper. The winner was one Levin Snivel, who sent in a palindromic poem of twelve octosyllabic lines. Sydney at once composed a poem of twenty decasyllables, and sent it to the editor, who published it with regrets that it had not been submitted in time for the competition. Snivel retorted with a poem of forty duodecasyllables; Sydney countered with sixty of the same.

When Snivel produced a poem of a hundred fourteen-syllabled lines, Sydney felt the time had come to take decisive action. He conceived the idea of the palindrome to end all palindromes. He would write a full-length palindromic novel to be entitled "D'neeht." He began work on the project right away.

A small but sufficient legacy enabled him to retire from book-keeping and devote all his time to writing. He toiled day and night, pushing away untasted the meals Edna brought to him. Ultimately she left him, taking young Edna with her. He never noticed their absence; they had each given him an andedna, all he wanted, all he would ever want, from them.

At last, after thirty long years, we heard that "D'neeht" was completed. Wordrow and I were invited to the garret where Yendys now lived, to view the finished product. We ascended the stairs at the appointed hour of midnight, and found the palindromist celebrating the occasion with a roaring fire in the grate and a glass of newly-bought whiskey in his hand. He poured two glasses for Wordrow and myself, urging us before we drank to gaze upon the completed typescript. With a tall candle burning at each side of it, it lay upon a small table, open at the middle page, with the central, pivotal sentence of the colossal palindrome underscored heavily in red. "D'neeht" was (so Yendys had told us) an anti-war novel; into the pivotal sentence, appropriately enough, was condensed the essential theme, the message, of the book.

Reverently we approached the table and gazed upon the type-written pages. The sentence underlined in red was, naturally, the first that caught our attention.

"Snug and raw was I," we read, "ere I saw war and guns."

I gazed (like Edgar Allen Poe) mute, motionless, aghast! A glance to one side told me that in the same moment Yendys had seen the fatal, hitherto undetected flaw. His lips quivered, his lower jaw dropped, perspiration bedewed his brow. A glance to the other side told me that even Wordrow (who was never very bright) had spotted it also.

A brief inspiration, lasting merely a moment, came to me. "An ampersand!" I cried. "That's all you need! Simply make it 'Snug & raw was I ere I saw war & guns.'"

The words died on my lips even as I uttered them. To a palin-dromist of Yendys' artistic integrity, such a miserable, makeshift compromise would, I knew in my heart, be utterly impossible. A chain can never be stronger than its weakest link. The labor of thirty years had been in vain.

With a shuddering sigh, Yendys picked up his typescript, pressed his lips to it, steadily carried it across to the open grate, and flung it on the fire. It was typed on sheets of di-olullectical acit-celluloid, and therefore was consumed immediately.

Yendys then produced an automatic pistol, pointed it at his temple, and pressed the trigger. So he sank, deep into the dark abyss of endless d'neeht.

A memorial service was held in the United Free Anagrammarian Church, of which Yendys had for many years been a member. The minister, the Rev. Ernest Sterne, author of the celebrated anti-Episcopalian tract, *Ye Slew Wesley*,* preached on a text from John Donne: "When thou has done, thou hast not done." Later, on Yendy's tombstone, a line from Eliot was carved: "In my end is my beginning."

* [Author's Note: Dr. Sterne's *Ye Slew Wesley* (an anagram, but unfortunately only a near-palindrome) is itself symbolic of frequent failure among palindromists. —HWB.]

Sotadic Verses,
Sacred and Satanic

Palindromes have a special magic which is all their own, just as do music, mathematics, the moonlight, the lost art of banister-sliding, making mud-pies, playing the stock-market, and love's first kiss. The combination of reversibility and intelligibility has a peculiar power of conferring, seemingly, upon the palindrome a veritable intelligence of its own. In this connection, it is interesting to examine a triad of reversible English words which generate about themselves a preternaturally luminous aura. The words express in a simple, yet thoroughly general way that which can only be called the fundamental moral injunction; then—shockingly, by virtue of their reversibility—they announce the same's indubitable corollary. One may say—a bit poetically—that the three words (as read from left to right) embrace Kant's "moral law within" us and the teaching of The Prince of Peace:

Deliver no evil.

The corollary (revealed in the reversal) is, to be sure, not anything that anybody particularly wants; but it states precisely what any person who would obey the law *must be prepared to withstand*, to wit: all the rigors of this world—the oppressor's wrong, draughts of hemlock, or crowns of thorns. Such was the corollary taught by precept and example (and here it is appropriate to vary the sobriquet) by The Man of Sorrows:

Live on reviled.

Note that while the law and its corollary, being mutual reversals, are inseparable orthographically, they are also, with respect to their meanings, inseparably the same teaching (just as The Prince of

Peace and The Man of Sorrows are one and the same teacher), since to heed the one is necessarily to heed the other.

Deliver no evil; live on reviled.

A religious zealot, finding in this sentence's reversibility a sign of the presence of the man who was its personification, might regard it as the logological harbinger of the Second Coming; a religious mystic might find revealed in its orthographic symmetry the miracle of The Word Made Flesh become The Flesh Made Word; a devout theologian might view its six words as a providential combination of fearful eschatological portent; and even a highly suggestible, non-materialistic philosopher might recognize in its *palindromicity* a heraldic emblem of Divine Authority, a credential of Transcendent Origin.

Among the collected palindromes of Edwin Fitzpatrick, there is one in particular which reads quite as though some other-worldly influence may have presided over its conception. It has been otherwise interpreted. Some have thought it had to do with the War of the Roses which lasted until 1485 when Henry Tudor assumed the crown of England; others have tried to relate it to the tragedy of *Romeo and Juliet*. But a third theory holds that it refers to the Crucifixion, and to an unrecorded defender of Jesus—a woman, evidently—who did not flee with his other friends, but who stayed with him and tried to plead (in the first couplet) with the arresting officer in his behalf. The officer, adamant, replied (second couplet). The third person to speak was Jesus. Finally, according to the palindrome, the woman (desperately) spoke again, urging flight:

> "Revolt, Capitano? No!
> I tag it: 'Sacred Rose of Red.'"

> "No! We talk lawsuit.
> No petal, I presume, rips a dogma."

> > "I deliver storied, sung, Astral Aid.
> > O, profit on droll anger? Regnal Lord, not I!
> > For podial arts Agnus Dei rots.
> > Reviled I am, God."

> (Aspire, muser!
> Pilate, Pontius, walk late—wonder! . . .)

> "Foes order castigation!
> On a tip act, Lover!"

Sometimes Fitzpatrick was an instrument of the Light, sometimes of the Darkness. He suffered from a chronic Nita-Natasha fetish—Nita because her name occurs in reverse in hundreds of English participles, Natasha because of her association with Satan. Often he burned the midnight oil, glibly composing palindromes about them (and other girls); the next day he would present them to his class, usually prefacing the results of the night before with an equally glib lecture (I have room for only a sample):

> I will try to elucidate for you, with all my sophistry—and subterfuge—mine own philosophical bent concerning some orthographic forms of poetry which are, indeed, matters of letters.
>
> Palindromic poems have a credibility or incredibility very similar to the apparent facts of the mind-body riddle. Philosophers are forever asking: how is it possible for the Mind, which appears to have no similarity, in its principles, laws, structure—indeed, in any way at all—to the Thing the physicists are so feverishly studying, to inhabit this utterly dissimilar thing—this "matter," to accommodate itself to its irrelevant and obstructive ways, and to even become one with it for a time? A like question could be asked about palindromes, for here the letters are orthographical atoms analogous to the physical atoms of our bodies, out of which the "body" of the palindrome is assembled, and throughout which sprawls its "soul," or meaning, just as if no home more comfortable or well-suited to its needs could possibly be devised. But these letters obey a law of symmetry, and, except that it is a simple single law, and a known law, it is entirely analogous to the laws of physical atoms; it is a law irrelevant to, obstructive to, and unrelated to the entirely different laws of grammar, logic, drama and dreaming which govern those utterly different, quasi-living mental things called meanings; and it is a law which is indifferent to the collective élan or compulsion of those meanings to orchestrate themselves into unity with the orthographic atoms—so as to become an embodied soul.

Four of Fitzpatrick's poems, composed of a total of eighteen (numbered) palindromes, follow.

Elegy on the Death of Sister Nita and Her Cat, Bigot

(1)   I saw a lone Bigot live.
Live now shall a hoar bedside idyll.
A cigar to senile fatso? Lemon, Amoret?
Aloe, cruel bailiff?
A nun, Adine, I saw alone. Bigot, live—live now!
(Shall a hoar bedside idyll?)

A cigar to satinet, aloe-cruel bailiff—Anubis!
Naomi, stark rabid, I bark "Rats!"
I moan, Sib!
Unaffiliable urceolate Nita so tragically died!
Is Debra (Oh Allah's won!) evil—evil to gibe, Nola?
Was I, Enid?

An unaffiliable urceolate Roman (O me!)
Lost a feline, so—tragically died!
Is Debra (Oh Allah's won!) evil—evil to gibe?
Nola, was I?

An Apostle in Flight Shakes His Fist from a Safe Distance

(2)   Eva, hot Ma, I sail amid arrests!
       I go, Lois, ere heresiologists err!
       A dim alias I am to have.

(3)   Snug senile Heresiologist, farce!
       Be xerus-nosed, aha!
       (Hades! On sure xebec-rafts I go, Lois, ere he lines
          guns!)

Cold Ewes

(4)   Debase wedlock, cabaret tuba.
       Hades! A bed a fire wolfed!
       So—did ye know, Eva, his pilar bed?
       Sex of lepers nor pariahs, aloof, debase wedlock;
       Cold ewes abed, Naomi, debase.

       Ye kiss, I know, Eva, his pilar bed foliated mossily
       (Sordid Norah's goldenrod-adorned log).
       "Sharon, did rosy lissom detail of Debra—
       Lips I have won—kiss Ike?"
       "Yes—abed!" I moan.

       Debase wedlock, cold ewes abed.
       Fool! As hair aprons repel foxes,
       Debra—lips I have won—key didos deflower,
       If a debased Ahab utter aback
       Cold ewes abed.

Nita Lulu Meets the Father of Lies

(5)   Ah Satan, dog-deifier! (*Oh who reified God, Natasha?*)

(6)   Dog-deifiers reified God!

(7)   (*Lattimer asks a remittal, Eva.*
       Histolytic city lots I have; Lattimer asks a remittal.)

(8)   Ah Satan, shall a devil deliver Hannah?
       Reviled lived Allah's Natasha!

(9)   (*Moo, lost elk, O orbs amid wonders awed!*
       Was it organic, in ecstasy tied, Deity sat scenic in a grot?
       I saw dew as red—now dim as brooklet—so loom.)

(10)   Ah Satan, no smug smirk rims gums on Natasha.

(11)   (*Emma, doll, I'd accept Nan Guper as a ton tub—*
       But not as a repugnant peccadillo, dam me!

(12)   *Ramona is reposed in a nide so Persian, Omar.*

(13)   *Sal, a late petal up in a mill I manipulate—petal alas!*

(14)   STAB, MOW, KNIFE DE FINK WOMBATS!)

(15)   Did I, ameliorating Nita, roil Ema? I did.

(16)   Did I, debating, Nita dating, Nita bed? I did.

(17)   Degenerating, I do maim—assail, alienating Nita.
       I came, fleecing Nita—I *dare* ululating Nita.
       Rape's era now is gelatinating; Nita, I've done no
         deviating.
       Nita! Nita! Legs I won are separating!
       Nita Lulu—eradiating nice elf—emaciating Nita,
       Neil, alias *Sam*, I am! O dig?
       (Nita reneged!)*

(18)   (*Ah, Satan, derogating Nita, hating Nita, gored Natasha.*)†

---

* What girl wouldn't have, after hearing a line like that?

† If it was really Nita he hated so much, why did he gore Natasha? To such questions as this, and many others—such as "Why did the horde of wombats suddenly attack the Dark Philandering Angel?" we probably never will know the answers; but naturally, for deception's sake and concealment, Satan resorts to the Sotadic mélange.

Vocabularyclept Poetry

or Mathematical Collaboration

Palindromes and charades suffer from the defect that the vocabulary available to them is severely limited. Indeed, most words cannot be used in either palindromes or charades at all. A most desirable innovation would be a form of composition as neat and appealing, as difficult and challenging, as are palindromes and charades, but in which any word would have as much chance to be used as any other. If only someone could find such a dragon, we could all try to slay it.

Recently a mathematical mode of collaboration having some of the earmarks of such a dragon has revealed a new dimension of most poignant interest in poetry—that patient over which many doctors despair.

When a poet organizes significant sounds into poems, he engages in an activity which may be analyzed into two activities which are discussed in algebra textbooks under the familiar names: combinations and permutations. The poet selects one combination of words out of an infinite number of possible combinations. Simultaneously, he imparts to these words one permutation out of a finite but very large number of possible permutations. But, although the poet does both things together, it is imaginable that they could be done sequentially; the combination could be completely chosen first, and the permuting done afterwards. The writing of a poem could be divided into two parts—the first poet selecting the combination of words and the second poet permuting the words into a poem.

One way to select a combination of words for the purpose is to take a poem which has already been written in the old hat way (it is best not to have a complete break with tradition), and then dissolve the poem by arranging all its words in a single alphabetical order.

This list may then be given to another poet whose task it is to reconstruct the words into a poem.

An interesting upshot of all this is that it provides a means by which the living can collaborate with the dead. A one hundred-word poem by Walt Whitman, given below, will serve to illustrate this. It is followed by another and considerably different poem which is nothing but a thorough reshuffle of exactly the same one hundred words.

Poets to come! Orators, singers, musicians to come!
Not today is to justify me and answer what I am for,
But you, a new brood, native, athletic, continental, greater than
    before known,
Arouse! for you must justify me.

I myself but write one or two indicative words for the future,
I but advance a moment only to wheel and hurry back in the
    darkness.

I am a man who, sauntering along without fully stopping, turns a
    casual look upon you and then averts his face,
Leaving it to you to prove and define it,
Expecting the main things from you.

                                     —*Walt Whitman*

Is it One I am from, or Two?
Brood a moment, but, before you answer,
You and I must justify it,
For I myself am leaving you.

The athletic man turns his wheel to advance upon the casual main,
And then but averts you—
You sauntering native singers without the continental look—
To come back to things known;

But I who face a fully indicative darkness,
Stopping not for what orators prove to me,
Expecting only today to come along new,
Hurry—and write a poet's words
For a future (greater than musicians arouse and define in me!)
To justify.

                                     —*Whitman–Bergerson*

It seems reasonable that vocabularyclept poems should be signed first by the poet of combination and second by the poet of permutation, since combination necessarily precedes permutation.

The first vocabularyclept poem ever composed was constructed "blindly." This remarkable feat was managed by J. A. Lindon, who worked from the 478-word list shown below, without any knowledge of the original poem, and without even knowing its title or author.

I   a a a a a a ache
ago ah all all all all all
all all all all all alone alone alone
alone always an an and and and
and and and and and and and
and and and and and and and are are
are are as as aspirations away away bakes bark battle
be be be be before before being beings bland blast blazed
blow bread build burnt but but by
came can can candle candle cannot charred chimney clean
    coal-oil

II   coat comforted come couch crude crystal darkness days death
    determination did
die done doubt downward driving dusk dusk eat eaves elbow
    eternity excelled except
exists failing failing falls fate fate fed feel felt
few filled finish fire first flies floss found for for forgiven forever-
    receding from

III   future gloaming glow go gods goes gone grates grow hand
hardship have head heartless heaven here here hold human
human hunger hurry I I I I I
I I icicles ideal if if imaginary in
in in in in in in in in in infinity into is
is is is is is it it it it it

IV   it it it kalaidoscope knot lamp lamp late least
less lesser lighted lighted lilt listening loaf lonely long long
looking lost love love low lying magnanimous may
me me me me me me me meant melt
memory men mind mind months moving mud music
music musk must must my my my
my mystic nearly nearly never night not not

V   not now nowhere ocean of of of
of of of of of of of of of of
of of old on on on one
only only only only or
out out out oven own pain pains partly

perhaps perhaps pitch plunge quilt rain reach remember
    resolute riving
rose said sends see see seeings short shall shall shall
should should silence sinks

VI   sit slightly slow snow snow snow
snow snow snows so so something
sooner soul soul soundless split stand still stove strain
such swirling take takes
than that that that that that that that that
the the

VII   the the the the the the the the the
the the the the the the the the the
the the the the the the the the the
the the the the the the the the the
the the the the theme then then

VIII   there these they things things this this though though
thoughts through through through through through thud thy
time tinsel to to to to to tragedy trees under
universe up upon vain vain veins venal versed walls was
was watch watery watery we we we
weaves were were were wet what when when while
whirl white will will will windowpane wind's

IX   winter with with with with with with without
women wood world world worlds would would wrong yellow
yes yet you you you you you
you you you your your your your

To orchestrate such a long list of pre-chosen words into a poem undoubtedly poses an intimidating problem. Mr. Lindon's account of how he set about it is fascinating:

First I cut the necessary 500 odd slips of cardboard and wrote the words on them, then put them in a shallow tray with lettered compartments. Then, having taken some days doing this, I scrapped the idea as hopeless! I should never have been able to find the words I wanted quickly enough, should never have known what was available. So I made out a second alphabetically ordered list, like your own (which I wanted to leave untouched for reference) and worked from this, blacking out any words I used as I used them. My starting idea was to pick out those words used twice (or more often) and separate them into two batches, one for the opening stanza, one for the final stanza, so as to get some sort of unity at the ends, so to speak. In the event, however, alterations distorted this idea out of all recognition. But I did get a goodish opening stanza and an equally good final one. And a second stanza and a penultimate one. And, in fact, others in-between, until only two remained to do. Then the screw began to turn! I found myself left with a quite hopeless jumble of words, 16 the's, 8 it's, all the me's, lots of shall's, will's, should's, and so on—useless for making anything at all. I suppose our styles of writing caused this, a difference of density, a degree of compression of material. So, miserably, I had to go through it all, removing good phrases like "Night is an ocean of pitch" and replacing them with mere emptinesses, heart-breaking! This gave me some material for my two remaining stanzas, but so far random material only. I shuffled some of it into something like sense (or nonsense) and then made a second raid on my already written parts to obtain such words as were necessary to finish off what was done in rough only. For this latter part I did use my pieces of cardboard, so the labour of making them was not entirely wasted; but it would have been quicker to make only a number of blanks and write such words on them as were needed at this late stage.

Finally I got all the words shuffled in somehow, with tolerable results; but oh how wretched were all my excellent earlier stanzas by this time! I spent about a week trying to improve the whole poem, but this certainly takes time since one word cannot usually be put in instead of another simply using a straight switchover; if word A would improve the effect at B, word B won't usually go in at A, but might possibly (if . . .) go in at C, and so on. One could spend weeks at this without much change.

Well, I send you the result. It does make some sort of sense and, like genuine poetry, does seem to have elusive undercurrents of meaning.

I took the liberty of giving Mr. Lindon's reconstructed poem the same title as I had given my original. J. A. Lindon's reconstruction follows:

Winter Retrospect

I   Night sends me this whirl of snow.
Under the low trees the watery glow
Of your lamp looking through the dusk—my
Thoughts are still that it must die.
Upon these walls the snow is driving.
Grow with the wind's lonely music, my soul, riving
Bland aspirations split with the blast up in the eaves,
And I shall remember only that the mind, though failing, weaves
Tinsel in darkness, memory a kaleidoscope, floss
That soundless flies, musk rose, and all that nearly was.

II   You and I were always alone, excelled only in resolute seeings
Of fate found in the crystal gloaming and fed on silence,
    mystic beings;
You and I through rain would watch forever-receding
    infinity,
You and I would see in the snow things that must never be.

III   Head sinks from hand to elbow. Lying on my quilt
Listening—is it the couch, is it the lilt
Of music?—I battle with the universe, long
For a few men less heartless, human wrong
And all the ache of the human mind and the soul forgiven.
Here now are the gods; nowhere but here is heaven.

VI   If only all were venal! Ah, we are versed
In thy theme as worlds plunge downward with the first
Imaginary thud of the lost ideal, something we
Have not done, though the world did, so watery
And vain the slow knot of the veins,
Short of determination, all alone, and partly
That it perhaps cannot reach with lesser pains.

V   Being the least of things, you should
Hurry through the lighted world as through a charred wood.
Eat bread before the lamp goes out,
While you can finish it.
What long ago exists? Then take you hold
Of this late coat of pain before, with months, old
Winter falls away; sooner than stand the strain, be filled
With fire and build.

VI   Yes, we were so nearly it,
Were perhaps not meant to doubt.
Can I love your failing me, and the tragedy?
Was the white all
Yellow when, the candle lighted, you came to see
But candle?

VII   May your will be the if and should, go
Swirling me there alone when the snows shall blow
Away through an ocean of pitch. Shall the snow
Be then your will, the only will come out
Of all the future said of it?

VIII   An eternity is burnt on the stove that takes
Coal-oil. For me, crude in the oven bakes
A loaf. And clean bark in the grates. I felt
It slightly comforted me. Snow gone, and the icicles melt.
One time all the chimney blazed, yet
Fate is magnanimous: not a death or a hardship except
Moving out into the mud and wet.

IX   They sit me in the dusk by the window-pane
To feel that all my days are in vain
Without you of all women to own
And love me. Such hunger, all alone.

—Bergerson–Lindon

It should be noted, when comparing, that Mr. Lindon in his reconstruction used the same number of words in each line and the same number of lines in each stanza as were in the original. The opening stanzas of the two poems have an amazing similarity. In each case it is the opening stanza which sets the stage. One can only wonder at the number of words common to both No. I stanzas: sends, whirl, snow, under, trees, watery, glow, dusk, walls, snow, driving, soul, riving, bland, blast, eaves, only, failing, weaves, tinsel, floss, soundless, musk.

It is of psychological interest that the original was written in January, 1944, by a twenty-one-year-old American, and the vocabularyclept reconstruction in January, 1969, by a fifty-four-year-old Englishman.

Winter Retrospect

I   Blow, blast. Whirl through the dusk, snow,
Downward swirling, then into the trees go.
Short is the gloaming, long thy soundless driving.
Coat the tinsel icicles under my eaves.
Hurry your failing glow to my window-pane.
Build up the slow ache in me that rain
Cannot. Only the snow the soul of winter is riving,
Only the snow the soul of me. Only the snow weaves
That watery crystal floss filled with dusk
And sends through the walls that bland and watery
    musk.

II   The fire is nearly out. The wood is low—and wet
With bark and veins of white pitch—split in the snow and
    mud.
The coal-oil sinks. The lamp is not out yet.
In the stove a charred knot falls through the grates with a
    thud.

III   I must clean the lamp chimney. In the oven bakes
A loaf of crude bread, burnt perhaps, but takes
That lesser hunger with it when it goes.
It must be nearly done, it slightly rose,
Ah yes, it did—I shall sit and eat it all alone.
Were you here with me it should be sooner gone.

IV   Were you here with me, you would finish first
And watch me, lying on the couch, your yellow head
Upon your hand, your elbow on the quilt.
Few are the things I remember that you said.
Perhaps you were comforted to see me fed,
Though being only in the silence versed
Or listening to the lost wind's lonely lilt.

V   I was alone before I found you,
Alone in all this world of hardship and of pain,
Of heartless men and venal women vain.
I was alone and meant
To battle all and one with resolute determination.
And then from out the darkness a lighted candle came
And a strain of music. You were the lighted candle,
Love the magnanimous theme.

VI   But the you of long ago
Now exists nowhere in the universe
Except in the vain world of my own mind
As a forever-receding imaginary,
Always before me moving, blazed on the mystic night,
Looking away.

VII   If these are not the pains that human beings
Can stand, can hold the least, would die without,
In my mind there is something less than doubt.
All thoughts of death, all music, and all seeings,
In the memory of love, are tragedy.

VIII   The time may never come, and if so, late,
When we shall have excelled an old ideal.
The days will grow to months, the snows will melt,
And such as I will still feel what we felt.
So flies the kaleidoscope of human fate
Through all the future, while all the worlds that be
Plunge away through an ocean of infinity.

IX   For this the gods of fate should be forgiven,
That they are partly wrong, not all things see,
And by failing aspirations reach we heaven
Though it shall take for all eternity.

                            —Howard W. Bergerson

In the May, 1970, issue of *Word Ways: The Journal of Recreational Linguistics*, Dr. A. Ross Eckler published a statistical study of the two Winter Retrospects, entitled "Anagramming One Poem into Another." Dr. Eckler's article is reproduced below.

In the February, 1969, issue of *Word Ways*, Howard Bergerson dissected a poem into an alphabetical list of 478 words and invited readers to construct a new poem out of this raw material. One reader—J. A. Lindon—took up the challenge, and in the next issue of *Word Ways* the original poem and the reconstruction were presented simultaneously.

It is interesting to examine these two poems in detail, noting their points of similarity and their differences. Is the reconstructor inevitably forced to create much the same poem as the original, or is he likely to come up with an essentially independent creation? In other words, to what extent is the content of a poem dictated by the stockpile of words which it uses?

To assess the similarity of two poems is decidedly a difficult and a subjective task. To what extent have Bergerson and Lindon conveyed the same message to the reader? The first two lines of their respective poems possess a remarkable similarity, introducing the concepts of darkness, snow, motion and trees:

        Blow, blast. Whirl through the dusk, snow,
        Downward swirling, then into the trees go.

        Night sends me this whirl of snow.
        Under the low trees the watery glow.

A cursory examination of the poems reveals that both authors associated the adjective *lighted* with the noun *candle* (Bergerson does it twice), and the adjective *heartless* with the noun *men*. Bergerson speaks of the *wind's lonely lilt*, and Lindon refers to the *wind's lonely music*. However, these are such natural associations that one should not be particularly surprised by the coincidence. On the other hand, the adjective *human*, appearing twice in the alphabetical list, ought to have a rather limited set of nouns to associate with (few authors would consider phrases such as *human quilt* or *human heaven*). Nevertheless, Bergerson comes up with *human fate* and *human beings*, but Lindon has *human mind* and *human wrong*. Similarly, Bergerson uses *charred knot* and *snows melt*, but Lindon prefers *charred wood* and *icicles melt*. One begins to wonder: is it possible that the two poems are really independent of each other, and the few coincidences to be ascribed to chance alone? (After all, when one throws a pair of dice, one expects to get a matching pair in one-sixth of the cases.)

This question can be settled only by taking a much larger sample of the words in the poems. Fortunately, Bergerson has made it relatively easy to compare the poems by insisting upon the condition that the reconstruction have the same number of words in each line and the same stanzas as the original. One measure of similarity is the following: if word A and word B are near each other in the original, one might expect word A and word B to be near each other in the reconstruction as well (although they could both occur early in one poem and late in the other). In other words, one can associate with each word a pair of numbers—the line in which the word occurs in Bergerson's original, and the line in which it occurs in Lindon's reconstruction. The words can then be plotted as points on a 57-by-57 grid (the number of lines in each poem); if the two poems are similar, one would expect clusters of such points to appear.

In order to make such plotting unambiguous, one must use words that appear exactly once in each poem. 159 of these words are listed below, together with their locations in the original and the reconstructed poems:

ache (6, 19), ah (19, 21), always (40, 11), aspirations (56, 7), bakes (15, 48), bark (12, 49), battle (32, 17), beings (42, 12), bland (10, 7), blast (1, 7), blazed (40, 51), blow (1, 43), bread (16, 30), build (6, 35), burnt (16, 47), charred (14, 29), chimney (15, 51), clean (15, 49), coal-oil (13, 48), coat (4, 33), comforted (25, 50), couch (22, 16), crude (16, 48), crystal (9, 12), darkness (33, 9), days (49, 55), death (45, 52), determination (32, 26), die (43, 4), doubt (44, 37), downward (2, 22), driving (3, 5), eat (19, 30), eaves (4, 7), elbow (23, 15), eternity (57, 47), excelled (48, 11), exists (37, 32), falls (14, 34), fed (25, 12), feel (50, 55), felt (50, 49), few (24, 18), filled (9, 34), finish (21, 31), fire (11, 35), first (21, 22), flies (51, 10), floss (9, 9), found (28, 12), forgiven (54, 19), forever-receding (39, 13), future (52, 46), gloaming (3, 12), glow (5, 2), go (2, 42), gods (54, 20), goes (17, 30), grates (14, 49), grow (49, 6), hand (23, 15), hardship (29, 52), head (22, 15), heartless (30, 18), heaven (56, 20), hold (43, 32), hunger (17, 57), hurry (5, 29), icicles (4, 50), ideal (48, 23), imaginary (39, 23), infinity (53, 13), kaleidoscope (51, 9), knot (14, 25), late (47, 33), least (43, 28), less (44, 18), lesser (17, 27), lilt (27, 16), listening (27, 16), loaf (16, 49), lonely (27, 6), lost (27, 23), low (11, 2), lying (22, 15), magnanimous (35, 52), meant (31, 37), melt (49, 50), memory (46, 9), men (30, 18), months (49, 33), moving (40, 53), mud (12, 53), musk (10, 10), mystic (40, 12), never (47, 14), night (40, 1), nowhere (37, 20), ocean (53, 44), old (48, 33), oven (15, 48), own (38, 56), pain (29, 33), pains (42, 27), partly (55, 26), pitch (12, 44), plunge (53, 22), quilt (23, 15), rain (6, 13), reach (56, 27), remember (24, 8), resolute (32, 11), riving (7, 6), rose (18, 10), sends (10, 1), seeings (45, 11), short (3, 26), silence (26, 12), sinks (13, 15), sit (19, 54), slightly (18, 50), slow (6, 25), snows (49, 43), something (44, 23), sooner (20, 34), soundless (3, 10), split (12, 7), stand (43, 34), stove (14, 47), strain (34, 34), swirling (2, 43), take (57, 32), takes (16, 47), theme (35, 22), thoughts (45, 4), thud (14, 23), thy (3, 22), time (47, 51), tinsel (4, 9), tragedy (46, 38), trees (2, 2), universe (37, 17), veins (12, 25), venal (30, 21), versed (26, 21), walls (10, 5), watch (22, 13), weaves (8, 8), wet (11, 53), whirl (1, 1), white (12, 39), window-pane (5, 54), wind's (27, 6), winter (7, 34), women (30, 56), wood (11, 29), worlds (52, 22), wrong (55, 18), yellow (22, 40)

What clusters of points actually occur? There are six word-pairs and one word-triple, summarized in the table below:

	Line on which the Word Group is Located	
WORD GROUP	ORIGINAL POEM	RECONSTRUCTED POEM
Heartless, men	30	18
lonely, wind's	27	6
lilt, listening	27	16
takes, burnt	16	47
bakes, oven	15	48
head, lying	22	15
elbow, hand, quilt	23	15

If all 159 words are plotted on a 57-by-57 grid, one cluster of points near (15, 50) immediately attracts the eye: crude, loaf, takes, burnt, bakes, oven, clean, chimney, stove, grates, coal-oil and bark. Obviously, these words have a strong relationship to each other which both authors may have exploited.

Are these clusters of points evidence in favor of the hypothesis that the two poems are, in some sense, similar? Or is it possible that the poems are completely independent arrangements of words, and the observed clusters no more meaningful than the groupings one observes of raindrops striking the pavement at the onset of a shower? To shed light on this question, each poem was divided into 15 sections of more or less equal size, each section (with one exception) being entirely contained within one of the original stanzas. The 159 words were then classified according to the section of each poem they were located in; for example, *window-pane*, located on line 5 in the original and on line 54 in the reconstruction, was assigned to section 1 in the original and section 15 in the reconstruction. In short, each word was placed in one out of 15 × 15, or 225, possible classes corresponding to its location in the two poems. The number of classes containing 0, 1, 2, ... words was then totaled up; the results are given in column two of the table below.

If the 159 words were independently arranged in the two poems (that is, if the relative positions of any two words in one poem has no effect on their relative positions in the other poem), statisticians can calculate (using the Poisson distribution) the typical, or average, number of classes that will contain 0, 1, 2, ... words. These average numbers are given in column three of the table below, and should be compared with the observed numbers in column two:

NUMBER OF WORDS IN CLASS	OBSERVED NUMBER OF CLASSES	AVERAGE NUMBER OF CLASSES
0	119	110.9
1	74	78.5
2	19	27.8
3	9	6.52
4	2	1.16
5	0	.166
6	2	.019
	225	225

The most striking disparity between columns two and three is contained in the seventh row. There, one sees that the actual number of classes containing six words is over 200 times larger than it should be if the 159 words were independently arranged in the poems! Rather than believe that Lady Luck has played such a monstrous trick on us, we prefer to believe that this is evidence of similarity between the poems—that is, that both authors made a conscious effort to use the words (bakes, oven, clean, stove, grates, coal-oil) in close association, and the words (quilt, hand, elbow, watch, head, lying) in close association. Note that one has already met seven of these words in an earlier table.

However, there is a further conclusion to be drawn. One concedes that the authors had very similar ideas about the use of these twelve words, but one must also conclude that, as far as the remaining 147 words are concerned, the authors bear no relation at all to each other. More precisely, the knowledge of how one author arranged these 147 words is of no help in telling us how the second author arranged them.

COMMENT (Howard W. Bergerson): The thing that surprises me most about this interesting statistical analysis is the fact that both poems have in common one quite palpable feature which appears to slip through the statistical net. Notice that the second stanzas of the two poems have scarcely any significant words in common. By contrast, the first stanzas have a large number of words in common. What I am wondering is: Is there any approach within the existing repertoire of the statistician which might enable him to assess the probability that the second author would select from the stock-pile so many of the same words to "set the stage" (which is what the first stanza does) that the first author used? The resemblance between the first stanzas is uncanny—even phenomenal.

About a year ago, Dr. E. N. Gilbert (of Bell Telephone Laboratories) said, "I was struck by the agreement of mood between the two poems. This must be the most convincing single demonstration of the influence of vocabulary on mood." Assuming that the alphabetical list induces a mood from the outset, and that this mood can be heightened by any one of many permutations of the words into a connected poem, one wonders just how different the moods of any two such permutations could be. Given an initial mood induced by the list, what is the probability that the mood will always direct certain words into certain ordained positions in the opening stanza of the poem?

REPLY (Dr. Eckler): Mr. Bergerson's observation is indeed confirmed by a statistical analysis similar to the one given above. Suppose that one divides the poem into 6 equal sections instead of 15, so that the first section is equivalent to the first stanza. If the two poems are random with respect to each other, about 6 out of the 159 words should appear in both of the first stanzas. One actually finds that 15 of these words appear in both of the first stanzas. Under the randomness hypothesis, the probability of 15 or more matched words is only .0013; I prefer to believe instead that some common factor, such as mood induced by vocabulary, is operating upon the two authors.

The results of a more elaborate experiment in poetic reconstruction were reported in the August, 1970, issue of *Word Ways*, in an article entitled "Three Poems from One Fountain." J. A. Lindon supplied Dr. Eckler and myself with the alphabetical word-list of a 338-word original poem, and we independently constructed new poems out of this material. This made it possible to compare the work of two authors, both of whom had worked with the same fixed stockpile of words, as well as to compare both reconstructions to the original. The experiment seemed to show that the Poet of Permutation has a very important role to play—and quite a bit of latitude in which to play it. The stockpile of words did *not* dictate a unique story, but many more or less equally plausible stories.

Dr. Eckler has expressed the fascinating suspicion that vocabulary-clept reconstructions may reveal more about the psychology of the reconstructor than about the original author. In short, he sees them as a sort of literary Rorschach test. (A striking confirmatory instance of this can be seen in the use made of the word "failing" in the first stanza of the Lindon-reconstructed "Winter Retrospect." It is highly unlikely that a very young person would have used the word in that way.) Yet the task of the poem-reconstructor cannot be entirely analogous to that of a person who is presented a Rorschach ink-blot and asked to describe what he sees in it, for the viewer of the ink-blot knows that the blot was never intended by anyone to represent some one particular thing, but the poem-reconstructor knows that the word-list is really a scrambled poem—and he may try to divine from the word-list just what the original poet's poem was about. These considerations, of course, suggest still other experiments. . . .

J. A. LINDON'S WORD-LIST

a a a a above adept
all alone always always always an and and
and and and and and and and
and and and and and around as
aside at at Auntie aware badge be be bear been
behind bills blank bold boots bow bright brown brunt
but but but buttons by can
can cannot certain
cheeks chocolate-cream chosen class collar colour comb confident credit
cuffs cup curls day day do doll-mascot drink edge enjoyed
error eyes failures family far figure final
first first flamed for for for for from
from front girls glee gloating goes
gold grew had had has have he
he he he he he hell here hero's
him him him his his his
home home I I I I I I I I
I I I if
imp impresario in in in in ineptitude
inward is is is it it
it it jam-pudding jersey
lace last late learnt leave leaving left
light like lunch mantelpiece marching me me
me mincepie mirror mocked money more much must my
my my my my my myself myself
neat Nell not now now now of of of of
of of of of of
old on on on on one
one one only pale parlour
part pepper-pot perhaps pick plainly
planted play playground's point
prizes pushed put quaint rebuffs

recall recollection remembered role run saving
say school seated see see see
seems shall she shelf shoulder small so so
so so so so some something spending spring stage
stamping startled still stood stop suits
table table taking tall-windowed tells temper that that
that that the the the the the the
the the the the
the the the the the the
the the the the the the the the their
then there things this this those through till till
tiny titbit to to to to to to too
took trim unashamed undignified unknown untenanted up upon upon
    vanish
velvet wait was was watching watching were when
when while while white will wings with
with with with with won would yet

Presented below are two reconstructions followed by Lindon's original. The narrator of "Malaise" is an unhappy and persecuted young girl. The narrator of "Last Thoughts of the Outsider" is an old man recalling his boyhood.

MALAISE

I   He seems so adept and confident.
    So he has always been an impresario,
    And, while gloating on my failures,
    Took the credit and won the prizes.
    Boots stamping, unashamed of it, he had the hero's role to
        play!
    And I stood still in the wings,
    Watching him bow till he had left the bright stage light,
    And would see myself chosen for that part.

II   I, always the small imp with the pepper-pot temper,
    With tiny cheeks flamed through with colour,
    Remembered when the girls were marching to class
    For the first day of school—and their certain rebuffs.

III He pushed me to the playground's shoulder
    And, while taking the badge of gold on my jersey,
    Mocked my ineptitude.
    One can see that it suits him to spring at me like this,
    Till I, startled, run far from here.
    But this is so undignified.

IV   One error was to leave home and family.
Too late I learnt, it is hell to be alone.
My inward glee grew all the day, when I was home.
By the mirror, I comb my brown curls aside,
And recall neat Auntie Nell, so pale and white in front of
      the mantelpiece,
A quaint figure in buttons and old lace
With trim of velvet around the collar and upon the cuffs.
Seated there at the table for lunch, with a jam-pudding and
      a mincepie,
I enjoyed a drink from the cup upon the shelf above.
Then she put the final titbit of chocolate-cream on the table.
But now that tall-windowed parlour goes untenanted.

V   If I do not stop spending so much,
My money shall vanish, leaving only the bills behind.
Can I, so plainly aware that saving is unknown, wait for
      those things?

VI   But see! As of now, I cannot bear the brunt
Of his bold eyes watching point blank.
Have I perhaps planted something in his recollection?
It tells him yet more of myself.
First and last, some now say he will pick me up.
Must one be always on the edge—his doll-mascot?

                               —*Lindon–Eckler*

Last Thoughts of the Outsider

I   I cannot always and for always
Will the bright colour of planted things to stop
In the pale light of the first spring day.
It is only a while till I leave for the Unknown Front—
So be still. There has been much to recall:
My failures, perhaps; my first ineptitude. When small,
I—to my credit—had a home.

II   Now in inward recollection far I vanish—
Bow to him (the one chosen figure) as of old.
He stood so confident—he, so adept, and he, so bold.
So, I can see plainly on him the hero's badge
When spending the money upon bills, and saving gold.

III   Watching from the tall-windowed parlour above the school
A class of girls, neat in jersey suits
And curls and boots, marching around the playground's edge,
I won myself cuffs; and—more to the point—
By gloating on chocolate-cream at the table,
The brunt of his rebuffs.

IV   At last, for a day, he and his family left their home,
Leaving the tiny doll-mascot seated on the mantlepiece
Like some quaint impresario in the now untenanted stage
    and wings.
She mocked me with brown eyes—
For it seems I myself had to do the play!

V   Then I remembered my role and part was always—lunch!
I took my pick of the jam-pudding upon the shelf,
Enjoyed the mincepie titbit on the table with glee,
But—while taking those prizes—grew aware through the
    mirror
Of Auntie Nell behind me, watching.
Too late! My cheeks flamed! The temper of that pepper-pot,
So trim with velvet buttons and collar, white lace and comb,
Was certain hell.

VI   But shall the one his shoulder pushed aside
See *him* bear with, be startled of,
And put up with that stamping imp? Is this it?
Something tells me, "Wait and see." If he were here now,
He would say it is an error that I have not learnt
That one must drink from this final cup alone.
Yet I can but run, undignified and unashamed,
Till all goes blank.

                             —Lindon–Bergerson

USURPER

Still plainly can I see myself
In the parlour of my first remembered home
Planted like some doll-mascot on a shelf
Upon the table for the family comb
To be run through my curls—bright gold their colour.
I had on one of those brown velvet suits
With trim lace cuffs and collar
And my boots

Were white with small neat buttons. It is quaint
But I can *see* all this; not in the mirror
Above the mantelpiece, but from a point
Behind and to the left. Perhaps an error
Of recollection here, yet I recall
Watching that tiny figure, now with badge
(Class One) upon his jersey, late for school,
Marching alone around the playground's edge
As he had learnt to do; and one spring day
Of pale tall-windowed light
Stamping in temper on his lunch: mincepie
And chocolate-cream. I see him wait,
Gloating with inward glee,
Seated at table by my Auntie Nell,
Eyes on the titbit of jam-pudding she
Is saving till the last; then—imp of hell—
The pepper-pot! When first I grew aware
Of him I cannot say, but it seems certain now
That always he was there
Taking the credit and the bow
While I, his unknown impresario,
Stood watching from the wings,
For he was so
Much more adept at things,
So bold, so confident, so unashamed,
And if I pushed in front
Would vanish, leaving me with cheeks that flamed
To play my chosen role and bear the brunt
Of mocked ineptitude. He, always he,
Took home the prizes, won the girls, enjoyed
The spending of my money, while for me
Only the old undignified
Rebuffs, the failures and the bills.
So it has always been, and so it is
And will be till the day when something tells
Me I must put a final stop to this,
That now he goes too far, and I shall have
To shoulder him aside, pick up and drink
The hero's cup myself and, startled, leave
The stage untenanted, the part a blank.

—*J. A. Lindon*

J. A. Lindon has commented amusingly:

> Auntie Nell, poor dear, is not really flattered by either of your por-
> traits! She must have been still in her teens at the time, or very near it—
> *not* a quaint creature in lace and velvet! Yet Ross has: ". . . neat Auntie
> Nell, so pale and white . . . a quaint figure in buttons and old lace with
> trim of velvet around the collar and upon the cuffs." She perhaps ought
> to have been allowed to ruddify up a bit on that jam-pudding! While you
> make her a hell-tempered pepper-pot, despite her appearance "so trim
> with velvet buttons and collar, white lace and comb." There must be
> something about aunts that suggests all this. I have often wondered at
> the auntihood of uncles that they dare marry one!

Finally, before the curtain is allowed to fall on the subject of
vocabularyclept poetry, I must quote the following thought-provok-
ing passage from a letter from Dr. Eckler, dated May 13, 1970:

> I have carried out some analysis on the degree of resemblance among
> the three poems. First, I divided each poem into 13 sections of 26 words
> each and carried out analyses analogous to those described in the May
> issue. I found, as expected, that the poems were certainly not random
> with respect to each other. I am now trying to go a little beyond this
> observation (hardly a surprising one to a linguist, I suspect), and explain
> the degree of correlation to be expected. However, this appears to be
> very difficult to do. To illustrate my dilemma: it is clear that the con-
> straints of language almost certainly dictate the formation of the phrase
> Auntie Nell, but it is harder to measure the inevitability of such phrases
> as playground's edge, grew aware, inward glee, vanish leaving, cheeks
> flamed, tall-windowed parlour, and so on. I have an ill-defined feeling
> that there is some "standard" amount of correlation imposed by the
> nature of the English language and its grammar, its word-associations,
> etc. If this is the main effect, one would expect that all pairs of poems
> would exhibit a similar amount of correlation. On the other hand, if one
> postulates that the poem-reconstructors are independently attempting
> to read the mind of the original poet from a knowledge of the words that
> he used, then one would expect the two reconstructions to be somewhat
> more different from each other than either one is from the original poem.
> (After all, "similarity" must be measured in a very multi-dimensional
> space, and it is unlikely that you and I would both "approach" Lindon's
> thoughts from the same direction.)
> It is hard for me to either prove or disprove these hypotheses from the
> available data, partly because I don't have a very good measure of
> "similarity." You may be interested in the following analysis, however.
> For each pair of poems, one can identify different degrees of association
> of pairs of words (in the following, I consider only those words which
> appear exactly once in the word-list). For example, *grew aware* appears
> in both your poem and Lindon's; I call this a 1-1 direct pattern. Also
> you have *untenanted stage* and Lindon has *stage untenanted*; I call this a 1-1

reverse pattern. Wider patterns exist; for example, *spending the money* and *spending of my money* is a 2-3 direct pattern. I tabulate below, for each pair of poems, all patterns up to and including 3-3:

Number of Close Patterns in Pairs of Poems

		LINDON–BERGERSON	LINDON–ECKLER	ECKLER–BERGERSON
1-1	direct	5	3	4
	reverse	1		
1-2	direct	3	2	
	reverse		2	
1-3	direct	1		
	reverse		1	1
2-2	direct	2	1	1
	reverse			1
2-3	direct	1		1
	reverse	2	2	1
3-3	direct		1	1
	reverse			

By this (imperfect) measure, there is a suggestion that you and I are farther apart than either of us is from Lindon, but the data is too scanty for significance.

There are quite a number of triple coincidences which would tend to suggest that all three of us are influenced by "common" word-associations. Besides Auntie Nell, I note (*cheeks* that *flamed, cheeks flamed, cheeks flamed*), (*velvet* suits with *trim, trim* with *velvet, trim* of *velvet*), (*something tells, something tells, something* in his recollection? It *tells*), (*spending* of my *money, spending* the *money, spending* so much, my *money*), (*drink* the hero's *cup, drink* from this final *cup, drink* from the *cup*), and so on. Are there more of these triple coincidences than normal, given the double-coincidences in the table above? I don't know yet. . . .

Anagrams

OR
GREAT ART
(Ars Magna)

Anagrams, like palindromes, have a long history dating back to ancient times. They were invented by the Greek poet Lycophron in 260 B.C. A definitive work on the subject, placing it in historical perspective, would be necessarily huge.

In 1925 a book entitled *Anagrammasia*, containing about 5,000 anagrams, was published. Only two or three copies are known to survive. It was compiled by a gifted anagrammatist who signed himself "Amaranth." Amaranth wrote some introductory matter, but in the actual collecting and assembling he had the help of eighteen other people. I have learned but little about him. In real life he was a lawyer—surnamed Lovejoy—who lived in Pittsburgh and/or Cincinnati. Several years after *Anagrammasia* appeared, a supplement to it was published. By now, the supplement, too, is almost infinitely rare. Another tome on anagrams which appeared in some hallowed past was entitled *Biblia Anagrammatica*. I have very little information on it.

The vast extent of anagrammatical literature is surpassed only by its scattered and inaccessible obscurity. Not often, I am inclined to think, have many such volumes ever found their way into a single library. But it has happened at least once—for, obviously, the above are precisely the kinds of books that Poe spoke of when he told us how once upon a dreary midnight he pondered weak and weary over many a quaint and curious volume of forgotten lore. To a time-traveling bookworm, Poe's chamber would be second in interest only to the lost library of Alexandria. Could we but browse through such books as those, would there be anything missing from *these* pages that in *there* we could not find? Surely we would find the 800 anagrams an admirer once composed on the name of the mathematician, Augustus de Morgan; and undoubtedly we would come across a dusty, illuminated volume enclosing between its covers the matter referred to in this quotation from a letter written by Leigh Mercer:

> A great sentence for anagrams is "The Angel's Salutation," Luke, Chapter I, verse 28: "Ave Maria, gratia Plena, Dominus tecum." With U and V interchangeable, 3,100 anagrams have been composed by one man alone, Lucan de Vriese. Others have composed 1,000 on this sentence.

My purpose in this chapter is to document some of the most excellent work of many other, mostly non-contemporary individuals. Most of the anagrams presented below have previously existed in collected form only in the private files of a very few outstanding anagram collectors. My greatest debt is to Erik Bodin (whose pseudonym is "Viking"), of Norfolk, Virginia, who made me a most magnanimous gift of his entire, vast collection of anagrams authored prior to 1932. William G. Bryan, of Greenfield, Mass., also sent a long list of anagrams constructed in the years 1932 to 1936. Leigh Mercer sent still another anagram list; and other people, too, contributed to the general pool from which this selection was made. I have given all the data I have so far acquired concerning the author of each anagram and the date and place of its first publication. It seems to have been the custom among most practitioners of the art to use pseudonyms, and I regret that in most cases the reader will find only a pseudonym attached to the anagram. But, of course, to attempt to discover the real names and other biographical facts about so many, mostly nineteenth-century, people would be to embark upon a very considerable undertaking.

To separate a word or longer expression into the letters of which it is composed is to dissolve it semantically, since the letters are submorphemic units. To rearrange the same letters into a new expression related in meaning to the original, thus restoring something like the original content (but without restoring any of the original morphemes), is perhaps the most fascinating of the anagrammatical arts. The anagrams in the large group that follows are all of this kind—they stand in apposite relation to their subjects. The attentive reader will discover in the abundance of examples, here given, of this diminutive art-form—even as he would were he studying some lovely Golden Treasury of Japanese haiku—moments of rare and incredibly delicate beauty. Sources for anagrams are listed at the end of the book.

1. Abandon hope, all ye who enter here.
   Hear Dante! Oh, beware yon open hell.

2. Aboma.
   Am boa.

3. Absence makes the heart grow fonder.
   He wants back dearest gone from here.

4. Accentuation.
   I can cut a tone.

5. The accidental.
   Chance dealt it.

6. Action.
   A tonic.

7. Actions speak louder than words.
   Talk or airs can not show up deeds.

8. The active volcanos.
   Cones evict hot lava.

9. Actors.
   Co-star.

10. Adam and Eve.
    A man evaded.

11. Adapted.
    Dead pat.

12. Adelina Patti.
    Italian adept.

13. Admiral Richard E. Byrd Expedition.
    Hardy American explorer bid; did it.

14. Admirer.
    Married.

15. Adolescents.
    Enclose tads.

16. Adolf Hitler.
    Hated for ill.

17. Advertisements.
    (a) Items at venders.
    (b) I'm trades' events.

18. The Aesculapian.
    Heals acute pain.

19. Agamist [rare].
    I'm a stag.

20. Agnes Wickfield.
    Gal, Dickens wife.

21. An agrostologist.
    Got a' toil on grass.

22. An aisle.
    Is a lane.

23. An alarm clock.
    A lorn A.M. clack.

24. An alcoholic beverage.
    Gal, can I have cool beer?

25. Alexander the Great.
    General taxed earth.

26. Alienation of affections suit.
    I toot finis unto a false fiance.

27. The alligator.
    Lithe lagarto.

28. The almshouse.
    A homeless hut.

29. Alphabetically.
    I play all the ABC.

30. Alphonse Bertillon's measurement.
    Ear lobes thus tell prison men names.

31. Amanuensis.
A man's in use.

32. The amateur golf champion-
ship.
I, th' famous champ, get
hole in par.

33. The amateur thespians.
Inapt hams use theatre.

34. American.
Main race.

35. The American ambassador
of goodwill.
A dramatic solo woos Lind-
bergh a fame.

36. The American Indian.
I am in a thinned race.

37. The American Indian reservation.
It is one area red man can
thrive in.

38. America's cartoonists.
No artists are as comic.

39. Amerind.
Red man, I.

40. Amidships.
Maid's hips.

41. The ampersand sign.
Met reshaping "and's."

42. Anagrams.
Ars magna. [Latin for
"Great art."]

43. Anathema.
A man hate.

44. Anchoretism.
O, scan hermit.

45. Andersen's *Fairy Tales*.
Read elfs' yarns in a set.

46. Andrew Carnegie, the laird
of Skibo.
A braw kiltie and no greed
of riches.

47. Angered.
Enraged.

48. Animosity.
Is no amity.

49. Anopheles.
Ha! No sleep.

50. The answer.
Wasn't here.

51. The antique furniture store.
(a) A queer outfit turns in
there.
(b) Oft hunt queer treasure
in it.

52. Antique furniture stores.
Are in quest of utter ruins.

53. The Anti-Saloon League.
Let not ale-house again.

54. Apt.
Pat.

55. The Arabian Desert.
It's a heated barren.

56. The Arctic Circle.
Chart ice circlet.

57. The aristocracy.
A rich tory caste.

58. The Ark of the Covenant.
Noah voteth craft keen.

59. The artesian wells.
Water's in all these.

60. Articles of partnership.
Cite profit sharer plans.

61. Asininity.
Is inanity.

62. Aspersion.
No praises.

63. Asperity.
Yet I rasp.

64. The assassination of Huey Pierce Long.

Gyp! Chief Louisiana Senator seen shot.

65. The assassination of President Abraham Lincoln.
A past sensation chills me, or a fiend shot in a barn.

66. Asseveration.
As one avers it.

67. The Associated Press.
Has editor's set space.

68. As the twig is bent, the tree is inclined.
See treatise's intent: "Begin with child."

69. Astronomers.
(a) Moonstarers.
(b) On! More stars!

70. Athletics.
Lithe acts.

71. Atom bombs.
A mob's tomb.

72. Augustus De Morgan.
(a) Great gun! Do us a sum!
(b) Snug as mud to argue.
(c) O! Gus! Tug a mean surd!

73. The automobile radiator.
A tour made it heat or boil.

74. Aye.
Yea.

75. A balance sheet.
E'en a cash table.

76. The Banner of the United States.
Beneath the star I tenets found.

77. Bargain sale.
An aisle grab.

78. The Barmecide's Feast.
He bids me taste—farce!

79. A bartender.
Beer and art.

80. Bastard.
Sad brat.

81. Bathing girls.
In slight garb.

82. A bathing suit.
A snug habit, it.

83. Battle of Bunker Hill.
Earth-built knob fell.

84. The Battle of New Orleans.
Tell North foe was beaten.

85. The bayonets.
They stab one.

86. The beach resorts.
Bathers' cots here.

87. The Beatles.
These bleat.

88. The bed of Procrustes.
P's bed cut foe shorter.

89. Bedroom.
Robedom.

90. Beer saloons.
Boosers' lane.

91. Belligerents.
Rebelling set.

92. Beneath the sod.
Death, then so be.

93. Benedictions.
Cited benison.

94. Between Scylla and Charybdis.
Web scented, can hardly sail by.

95. Bewailed.
I.e., bawled.

96. Big mean huns.
Human beings.

97. The billiardist.
'Tis red ball I hit.

98. Billingsgate.
Is telling gab.

99. Blandishment.
Blinds the man.

100. The Blarney Stone.
Blather sent on ye.

101. Blatherskite.
Hi! Best talker.

102. Blithesomeness.
Best smile shone.

103. Boa constrictor.
Con it; cobra sort.

104. The Board of Aldermen.
Hard men after boodle.

105. The boarding house.
This abode o' hunger.

106. The boarding house mistress.
(a) Grub on her dish is mess to eat.
(b) Big Ida, she rents us the rooms.

107. Booker Washington.
Oh, negro knows a bit.

108. Borough.
Oho! Burg.

109. A bottle of whiskey.
It be thy flask o' woe.

110. The bottomless pit.
(a) Titles mobs' tophet.
(b) Hottest step—limbo.

111. The breweries.
Where it's beer.

112. Brigandage.
A big danger.

113. Brush.
Shrub.

114. The burial ground.
Dub ghoul terrain.

115. The burning of Ancient Rome.
Fire, mob, Nero chanting tune.

116. Burnishing.
Shining rub.

117. Burying the hatchet.
(a) Butchering thy hate.
(b) They curb the hating.

118. Caffraria.
Far Africa.

119. The California gold rush.
Fools hunt a real rich dig.

120. The cantakerous man.
Thus note a mean crank.

121. Capture of Ticonderoga by Ethan Allen.
Battle-hour glory cannot fade in peace.

122. Carcinoma of the breast.
A hot cancer bites a form.

123. The Cardiff Giant.
Cheat! I find graft.

124. The caricaturists.
Their art's caustic.

125. The Carnegie Library.
Be literary—charge in!

126. The Caroline Islands.
See coral in this land.

127. The carotid artery.
To carry heart tide.

128. Carrier pigeons.
Racing o'er spire.

129. Caste.
A sect.

130. Castle dangerous.
A Douglas's center.

131. Cast of characters.
Chart actors faces.

132. The Cathedral of Notre Dame.
Heart o' France modeled that.

133. The Cathedral of Rheims.
Her lot—famed arches hit.

134. Catherine de Medici.
(a) I did menace heretic.
(b) Her edict came in—die!

135. Cavern.
Carven.

136. The Census Enumerators.
These surname counters.

137. The centenarians.
I can hear ten "tens."

138. Charitableness.
I can bless earth.

139. The checkmating.
Theme: Catch King.

140. Chester Arthur.
Truth searcher.

141. Chesterfield, Camel, Lucky Strike, Old Gold.
Edict: Called corkers, smoke delightfully.

142. Chevalier D'Industrie.
A dicer, I hunted silver.

143. A Chinese restaurant.
Neat curt Asians here.

144. Christian.
Rich saint!

145. Christianity.
(a) I cry that I sin!
(b) Charity's in it.

146. Christmas time.
It charms mites.

147. Christopher Mathewson.
Oh, master pitcher shown.

148. The Cigar Store Indian.
A sign attired in ocher.

149. Ciphers.
Spheric.

150. Circumstantial evidence.
(a) Actual crime isn't evinced.
(b) Can ruin a selected victim.

151. The clandestine marriage.
A man, a girl, hit secret Eden.

152. Cleanliness.
All niceness.

153. Clothespins.
So let's pinch.

154. Clouds.
Lo, scud.

155. The cock and bull stories.
Cons both talk crude lies.

156. The cockroach.
Cook, catch her!

157. The collar buttons.
But can't those roll!

158. The college undergraduates.
Our "green" shall get educated.

159. A color scheme.
Em chose coral.

160. The Columbian Postage Stamps.
A batch to gum on a P.M.'s epistles.

161. Combination.
Mob in action.

162. The *Commentaries* of William Blackstone.
If thick treatise on common law labels me.

163. The coming Presidential Campaign.
Damn! Electing time is approaching.

164. Committees.
Cost me time.

165. Compassionateness.
Stamps one as so nice.

166. Compensations.
Pass coin to men.

167. Complexion beautifier.
I bemix pure face lotion.

168. Compound interest.
To do sum in per cent.

169. The compulsory education law.
You must learn; police do watch.

170. Condemnation.
I connote "damn."

171. A confirmed bachelor.
I face no bold charmer.

172. Conifers.
Cone firs.

173. Conservative.
Not vice versa.

174. The conservatories of music.
Some start fine voice chorus.

175. Considerate.
Care is noted.

176. Constantinople.
Point's not clean.

177. Consternation.
One cannot stir.

178. Constraint.
Cannot stir.

179. Contaminate.
Taint came on.

180. Contemplation.
On mental topic.

181. Contemplations.
Time to con plans.

182. Contradiction.
Accord not in it.

183. Conversation.
Voices rant on.

184. Conversationalist.
'Tis one vocal strain.

185. Conversationally.
Trains one vocally.

186. Co-ordinance.
In one accord.

187. Coquetries.
Quest o' rice.

188. Correspondents of the newspapers.
Corps penned press notes of the war.

189. Country lasses.
Coy artless 'uns.

190. The countryside.
No city dust here.

191. Court of General Session.
Scenes of rogues on trial.

192. The courtship of Captain Miles Standish.

This mad chap oft sent suitor in his place.

193. The courtship of Miles Standish.
(a) Deft suitor pinch-hits lass home.
(b) Other lithe chap suits fond miss.
(c) This fop Alden cour-teth his miss.

194. A coy debutante.
Beauty to dance.

195. The crater of a volcano.
Core for that lava cone.

196. Crenelation.
Let in no race.

197. Crime does not pay.
Damper on society?

198. Crinoline.
Inner coil.

199. Crocodile tears.
Cries do act role.

200. Curtailment.
Cut terminal.

201. The cuspidore.
He spit cud o'er.

202. Custard pies.
Cud pastries.

203. The customers.
Such met store.

204. Dail Eireann.
(a) An ideal Erin.
(b) I lead an Erin.

205. The daily classified advertisements.

Here vast lists cite if lady needs maid.

206. The daily newspapers.
We spy plain ads there.

207. The danger signal.
Let a red sign hang.

208. Daniel Boone.
In lone abode.

209. Daniel Webster.
Best law denier.

210. Dante Gabriel Rossetti.
Greatest idealist born.

211. The dawning.
Night waned.

212. Days of Auld Lang Syne.
Sunny gala days of eld.

213. Days of the Lenten Season.
No flesh eaten on set days.

214. The "Dead March" in *Saul*.

Hear deathland music.

215. The deadly nightshade.
Thing had deathly seed.

216. The deaf mutes' alphabet.
A set help the dumb—a feat.

217. Dealing on the square.
Things are done equal.

218. The death of Louis Kossuth, the Hungarian patriot-statesman.

This main knight o' southeast Europe hath found a rest at last.

219. The death of Robert G. Ingersoll, the famous agnostic.

Goes, a-gathering the belief that no Lord comforts us.

220. The death of Will Rogers and Wiley Post.

Hear sad words: pilot, wit gone, they fell.

221. Debutantes.
Bud at 'teens.

222. A decimal point.
I'm a dot in place.

223. Declaration.
An oral edict.

224. The Declaration of Independence.

(a) Can pen a nice old deed of thirteen.

(b) Oh, one clear defiant edict penned.

(c) A co-penned edict held nation free.

225. The defaulting cashier.
That sure hid a fleecing.

226. Deflated.
'Deed flat.

227. Degradedness.
Greed's sad end.

228. The Delaware River.
Hail, revered water!

229. Delegations.
Oiled agents.

230. Delicatessen.
Ensliced eats.

231. Denominate.
It named one.

232. The dentist.
Dints teeth.

233. Departed this life.
He's left it—dead—R.I.P.

234. Department stores.
Most trade present.

235. Depreciations.
No praise cited.

236. Deputy coroners.
Tend your corpse.

237. Desegregation.
Negroes get aid.

238. "The Deserted Village,"
by Oliver Goldsmith.
O, a gilded theme; bright
verses lively told.

239. Designation.
Is a denoting.

240. Desperation.
A rope ends it.

241. Destruction of Jerusalem.
Judea mourns for its elect.

242. Destructive western torna-
does.
Winds overturned oats,
trees, etc.

243. The detectives.
Detect thieves.

244. Dethroned.
Thro—ended.

245. Detour.
Routed.

246. Deviltries.
Tried evils.

247. The devotional songs.
A note hints God's love.

248. Diaper.
I drape.

249. The diatonic scale.
Teach in la, si, do, etc.

250. Dictionary.
Indicatory.

251. The Diplomatic Corps.
Chaps do politic term.

252. A dirigible balloon.
On big oiled air-ball.

253. The disaster at Martin-
ique.
Its marts are quiet in
death.

254. Discernment.
Mind's center.

255. Disconsolate.
Is not solaced.

256. The discovery of America.
Eve for historic day came.

257. Discretion.
Considerit!

258. Disintegration.
Darn it! It is gone.

259. A disordered mind.
So I did render "mad."

260. Disparagement.
Mean raps I'd get.

261. Disraeli.
I lead, Sir.

262. Dissimulates.
It misleads us.

263. Distillation.
Do it in a still.

264. Dissipations.
So I sit and sip.

265. The divorce of Josephine.
Jove sped no heir to chief.

266. Divorce scandal.
Love can discard.

267. A divorce suit.
I advise court.

268. Doctor Frederic A. Cook.
Crooked doer of Arctic.

269. Dolce far niente.
After indolence.

270. Dollar diplomacy.
A mad, droll policy.

271. A domesticated animal.
Docile, as a man tamed it.

272. Dormitory.
Dirty room.

273. The dramatic profession.
(a) Actors' hopes framed in it.
(b) And I act more for Thespis.

274. The dramatic representation.
Painted actors met in art here.

275. Dressed in a little brief authority.
Is feudal Briton's hereditary title.

276. Dromedarian.
A nomad rider.

277. The dromedaries.
Home—arid desert.

278. Dubitation.
A doubt in it.

279. Dynamite.
I may dent.

280. Earnestness.
A stern sense.

281. The ears.
Hearest.

282. The earthquakes.
That queer shake.

283. *The Eastern Enigma.*
Sheet great in name.

284. Eddie Cantor.
Actor, indeed!

285. Edge tools.
Good steel.

286. Edict.
Cited.

287. Edison incandescent lights.
Connected inside thin glass.

288. An editor.
Ad noter, I.

289. Editorial comments.
Moral items noticed.

290. Edwin Booth, the great tragedian.
Egad! I bowed at throng in theater.

291. Edwin Smith of Ardmore, Pennsylvania.
Every man find poser and his mail town.

292. Eerie voodoo rhythms.
They doom Hoover, Sire!

293. Egyptian cigarettes.
Ten gay petite cigars.

294. The Eiffel Tower.
Few flit o'er thee.

295. Eight square.
A queer sight.

296. The eighty-second convention of the National Puzzlers League.
Then feeling a huge devotion to puzzle in Hotel Casey, Scranton.

297. Eleemosynary.
Yes, ye almoner.

298. Election frauds.
Induce floaters.

299. Elephant's foot.
The plant of Eos.

300. Elevators.
Serve a lot.

301. Eleven + two.
Twelve + one.

302. The Emerald Island.
Ireland lads' theme.

303. Emotional insanity.
A loony taint is in me.

304. Emperor William Second.
Claims one world empire.

305. *The Encyclopædia Britannica.*
A dictionary can be elephantic.

306. Endearment.
Tender name.

307. England riots now.
Down, strange lion!

308. The Englishman.
"H" entangles him.

309. Enucleation.
Note in a clue.

310. Ephialtes.
Hit asleep.

311. The Episcopalian.
'Tis a chapel I open.

312. Episcopalianism.
Claim a pope is sin.

313. Epistler.
Repliest.

314. Epitomist.
I post item.

315. The equatorial regions.
A ring o' heat queers toil.

316. Eskimos.
Some ski.

317. Esprit de corps.
Pep's its record.

318. Eternal devotion.
I note ardent love.

319. Euphrosyne.
Super-honey.

320. The evangelist.
List! Get heaven.

321. Everlasting.
Vale! Resting.

322. An everlasting life.
Safe, eternal living.

323. Evil.
Vile.

324. An evil mind.
Devil in man.

325. Extenuating circumstances.
Can excuse giant crime stunt.

326. The eyes.
They see.

327. Fainthearted.
Hinted at fear.

328. Faintheartedness.
Then it sends a fear.

329. The fairy sprites.
Spirit fays there.

330. Faithless.
False, this.

331. Falsities.
Fit as lies.

332. Families.
Life's aim.

333. Fashion's decrees.
Chose a fine dress.

334. Fast Baker.
Breakfast.

335. Fathead.
A daft he.

336. Fatima.
I am fat.

337. The featherweight.
That wee fighter, he.

338. Federal Decoration Days.
A day enacted for soldiers.

339. The female impersona-
tions.
Here men fail not to ape
Miss.

340. Fiances.
Fancies.

341. "The First Apostle."
St. Peter's fit halo.

342. Five dollars.
I'd sell for a V.

343. A flame-throwing soldier.
I'd go to man wars' hell-
fire.

344. The flame-throwing
soldiers.
Those hold wars' melting
fire.

345. Flatteries.
False—trite.

346. Flirting.
Trifling.

347. Float.
Aloft.

348. Florence Nightingale.
Flit on, cheering angel.

349. Fluctuations of stocks in
Wall Street.
A little luck wins; fortunes
scoot fast.

350. The fool's paradise.
(a) False hope's road, it.
(b) Oaf's last dire hope.

351. The football games.
Gambol of athletes.

352. The forbidden fruit.
(a) Both fed; rift;
ruined.
(b) O, the duffer bit rind.

353. The Ford touring cars.
Tin roadster for chug.

354. Forester.
For trees.

355. A forged signature.
Great fraud goes in.

356. Forget-me-nots.
Fret me to song.

357. Fort Peck Indian Reservation.
A center of redskin privation.

358. Fortunate.
Turn o' Fate.

359. Fragile.
E.g., frail.

360. François de Voltaire.
I said, "O, France, revolt!"

361. French Revolution.
Violence run forth.

362. The frontiersman.
He tents on far rim.

363. A fruit and confectionary stand.
Fain can run to it for dates
—candy.

364. Fulton's steamboat.
Steam on; tub floats.

365. Galley slaves.
Gyves seal all.

366. The game of billiards.
Aim ball for this edge.

367. Garbage.
A beggar.

368. Garden of Gethsemane.
E'en God-man fags there.

369. Garnet, Amethyst, Emerald.
Three neat art gems, my lad!

370. The gendarme.
Armed gent, eh?

371. A gentleman.
Elegant man.

372. The German Kaiser.
A master king here.

373. The German soldiers.
Hitler's men are dogs!

374. Giant firecrackers.
Scaring fire-racket.

375. Gladiator.
A lad o' grit.

376. Gold and silver.
Grand old evils.

377. The golden days.
They gladden so.

378. A good name is better than great riches.
Be not a hoarder; right acts gain esteem.

379. A grade crossing.
Cars go; is danger.

380. Granate [obsolete word].
A garnet [modern word].

381. Grand finale.
A flaring end.

382. Gratitude.
Gude trait.

383. The great American desert.
I get a mere sand tract here.

384. The great New York rapid transit tunnel.
Giant work in street, partly underneath.

385. The green-eyed monster.
The ogre enters my Eden.

386. The grindstone.
Thins torn edge.

387. Grover Cleveland.
Govern, clever lad.

388. The guillotines.
I hit one's gullet.

389. *Gulliver's Travels* by Dean Swift.
Lets bully dwarfs, giants, revive.

390. A gypsy fortune-teller.
Gentry, spell your fate.

391. Hairbreadth escapes.
Death bares his crape.

392. Halitosis.
Lois has it.

393. Halley's Comet.
Shall yet come.

394. "Halt, girl!"
"All right."

395. Ham sandwiches.
Dish a man chews.

396. A hard-boiled egg.
O, haggard edible.

397. Harvesting season.
Save the grain, sons.

398. The headsman.
Death's man, he.

399. The headstones.
Deaths on these.

400. Hearthstone.
Heat's throne.

401. *The Heart of Midlothian* by Sir Walter Scott.
Cry in tolbooth; maid's wit freeth her at last.

402. Heights.
Highest.

403. Helicopters?
Pilots cheer!

404. Henry Wadsworth Longfellow.
Won half the New World's glory.

405. Hibernated.
Bear hit den.

406. Hibernates.
The bear's in.

407. Hibernianism.
Be in Irishman.

408. Higher mathematics.
M.A. teaches him right.

409. A highwayman.
Away! Hang him.

410. Hippopotamus.
Hi, pompous Pat!

411. Horatio Nelson.
Honor est a Nilo.

412. A horseless carriage.
So here is real gas car.

413. The hospital ambulance.
A cab, I hustle to help man.

414. Hotel to use.
House to let.

415. Houses of Parliament.
A pile for us on Thames.

416. The housewarming.
Thus rig a new home.

417. The humanitarians.
Hint Samaritan hue.

418. Humoristic cartoonists.
This on our comic artists.

419. Hustlers.
Let's rush.

420. The iceman.
I cheat men.

421. Iconodulist.
I count idols.

422. Identified.
I defined it.

423. Ignis fatuus.
Is it a fungus?

424. Ignorant.
No rating.

425. Impatient.
Tim in a pet.

426. Imperators.
A prime sort.

427. Impersonation.
Apers in motion.

428. The inauguration ball.
True union at a big hall.

429. Incendiarism.
Sin and crime, I.

430. In cold storage.
Cool trade sign.

431. Income taxes.
Exact monies.

432. Incompetents.
Inept men cost.

433. Incomprehensibles.
Problems in Chinese.

434. Inconsiderateness.
Is in sense "Don't care."

435. The incubator.
But hen actor, I.

436. In Davy Jones' locker.
No "Jack" lives yonder.

437. The Indianapolis Speedway Classic.
Indiana City so saw each speed spill.

438. Indian outbreaks.
A redskin in a bout.

439. Indigestible.
Edible? I sting.

440. Indomitableness.
Endless ambition.

441. Infantile paralysis.
Is an early spinal fit.

442. The inheritance tax.
An heir? Then exact it.

443. Innominate.
No name in it.

444. Innumerable.
A number line.

445. The insane asylums.
See a sly man shut in.

446. Insensate.
Anti-sense.

447. An inspired poet.
Spirit, pen an ode.

448. Insubordination.
Bad notions; I ruin.

449. Insurance policies.
Coin is in sure place.

450. Insurgent.
(a) Gets run in.
(b) I rent guns.
(c) Unresting.

451. Insurrection.
Ruction risen.

452. The insurrectionist.
He incites riot's turn.

453. Integral calculus.
Calculating rules.

454. Integrity.
Tiny tiger.

455. The International Cup Races.
Erin can't capture this alone.

456. In the gloaming.
(a) A mingle o' night.
(b) Main light gone.

457. In the South Sea islands.
A thousand islets shine.

458. An intolerable condition.
One ill I don't, I cannot, bear.

459. Intoxicate.
Excitation.

460. Intrusion.
Is to run in.

461. In union there is strength.
Herein the strong's in unit.

462. Investigators.
Great on visits.

463. Irate.
I tear.

464. The Irish nation.
Oh, is that in Erin?

465. The iron horse.
Ho! Here I snort.

466. Is pity love?
Positively!

467. Israel Putnam.
Salem Puritan.

468. Italian.
A Latin, I.

469. *Ivanhoe*, by Sir Walter Scott.
A novel by a Scottish writer.

470. Japan's earthquake disasters.
Shake Japs' quarters; dent Asia.

471. Jeanne d'Arc, maid of Orleans.
As a man, rejoined old France.

472. Jesus Christ, the savior of the world.
'Tis the just child who saves of error.

473. Jocundity.
Induct joy.

474. John Greenleaf Whittier's poems.
Impart herein the jewels of song.

475. The judgment day of the blessed saviour.
Jesus, thy advent so famed be our delight.

476. Juvenile delinquents.
Enlivened June's quilt.

477. Kleptomaniacs.
Task policeman.

478. Knee-brushes.
Bees' hunkers.

479. The knights of labor.
A bright honest folk.

480. Knights of the round table.
Bold hearts fought in Kent.

481. Ladies.
Ideals.

482. A lady's stocking.
Gal's dainty sock.

483. Lambaste.
Beat, slam.

484. Lamentations.
Listen at moan!

485. The last days of Pompeii.
Past homes of Italy pied.

486. The last roundup.
Lo! Death turns up!

487. Laundering.
Guard linen.

488. The law of self-preservation.
What a preventer of life-loss.

489. Lawyer.
Sly ware.

490. *The Lay of the Last Minstrel.*
This story that all men feel.

491. Lazy person.
No spry zeal.

492. The League of Nations.
Ah, late foes get union.

493. The Leaning Tower of Pisa.
(a) What a foreign stone-pile.
(b) A foreign heap tilts enow.

494. The Leaning Tower of Pisa, in Tuscany, Italy.
A funny spot in a sweet city; I o'erhang it all.

495. The legal profession.
Sole great help of sin.

496. The legislature.
I see legal truth.

497. Leprachaun [variant spelling].
Unreal chap.

498. A libel suit.
I'll sue a bit.

499. *The Life and Adventures of Nicholas Nickleby.*
Fine tale; find thou a novel by Charles Dickens.

500. Life insurance.
I rule finance.

501. The life insurance policy.
Lo, I help finance security.

502. Likeness.
Ilk's seen.

503. Limericks.
Slick rime.

504. A limited express.
I sped extra miles.

505. Lionesses.
Noiseless.

506. The lips.
Lispeth.

507. The liquor habit.
Quit! I rob health.

508. *The Literary Digest.*
Hit greatest dry lie.

509. The lodge ritual of initiation.
I unite; oft I ride goat into hall.

510. Long distance telephones.
Toll gained on speech sent

511. A long time between drinks.
Blanks on wet diet regimen.

512. The Lord's Prayer.
(a) Thy errors plead.
(b) Pester "Old Harry."

513. The lost paradise.
Earth's ideal spot.

514. Louise de la Valliere.
Led a Louis a live reel.

515. Love's young dream.
Go luny over dames.

516. Lowspiritedness.
Depression wilts.

517. Lubrications.
Oil acts in rub.

518. Lubrifaction.
Fact! Rub oil in.

519. Madam Curie.
Radium came.

520. The magic lantern slide.
Gleam entertains child.

521. Maine.
N.E. am I.

522. The Maine disaster.
Death is in steamer.

523. The manager.
Great man, he.

524. The manufacture of oleomargarine.
Mere outer change of our animal fat.

525. Many a true word is spoken in jest.
Men joke and so win trusty praise.

526. Maple sugar.
Real sap gum.

527. The marimba.
Hammer a bit!

528. Marriage.
A grim era.

529. The marriage ceremony.
O, my! A mere ring act here.

530. The married man.
I'm her darn mate.

531. Masquerade.
Queer as mad.

532. A masterpiece.
See me, I cap art.

533. The maternity hospital.
Type that mothers ail in.

534. Matrimonial.
Anti-immoral.

535. The matrimonial agencies.
I tie man's name to each girl.

536. Matrimony.
(a) Into my arm.
(b) I try? No Ma'm.

537. A mattress.
Mat as rest.

538. Measured.
Made sure.

539. Measurements.
Man uses meter.

540. The measures.
Meter has use.

541. The mechanical power.
Machine to help a crew.

542. Medical consultations.
Noted miscalculations.

543. The medical profession.
Find healers composite.

544. Mephistopheles.
(a) He, Sheol's pet imp.
(b) The hopeless imp.

545. A mercantile establish-
ment.
Able merchant met sales
in it.

546. *The Merchant of Venice*, by
William Shakespeare.
Hie where vain Shylock
pact meets female brain.

547. Merchant tailor.
Man art clothier.

548. A Merry Christmas and a
Happy New Year.
(a) Many a sad heart can
whisper my prayer.
(b) May many a red
wreath carry happiness.

549. Metaphysical sights.
Mystic shapes alight.

550. Metaphysicians.
Mystics in a heap.

551. Methodist.
The modist.

552. Metric system.
Mystic meters.

553. The metropolis of England.
'Tis London; ample fog
there.

554. The Metropolitan Opera
House.
Theatre to harmonious
people.

555. Midnight.
Dim thing.

556. Midshipman.
Mind his map.

557. Midwinter weather.
Wind, rime, wet earth.

558. Miguel Cervantes de
Saavedra.
Gave us a damned clever
satire.

559. Minaret.
Art in me.

560. Mince pies.
Spice in 'em.

561. Minus quantity.
Quaint tiny sum.

562. Minutes.
Sun time.

563. Mirage.
Imager.

564. Misanthrope.
Spare him not.

565. Mischief-maker.
Mark if I scheme.

566. Misfortune.
Oft ruins me.

567. A mispronouncement.
One can put misnomer.

568. Misrepresentation.
(a) Simon Peter in tears.
(b) Sir, am I not pretense?

569. Misrepresentations.
One interprets amiss.

570. Mistress Carrie Nation of Kansas.
A first-rate crankess on a mission.

571. A modern battle-wagon.
Let a gob tend man o' war.

572. Modulation.
I am not loud.

573. Molars.
Morsal.

574. The "Mona Lisa."
(a) Ah, I am stolen.
(b) No hat, a smile.

575. The monarch of the Persians.
He's competent Shah for Iran.

576. Monroe Doctrine.
"Come not in" order.

577. Monte Carlo.
Lancet room.

578. A monument.
On mute man.

579. Moonlight.
Thin gloom.

580. A moonlight serenade.
Maid e'en longs to hear.

581. The moonlight serenader.
No delight to men hearers.

582. Moonlight serenades.
(a) Then Romeos sing lead.
(b) Ah, sing me tender solo.
(c) Hear olden time songs.

583. The morning star.
Near night's mort.

584. A morphine addict.
Man hit acrid "dope."

585. The Morse code.
Here come dots.

586. Mosquitoes.
O, Moses! Quit!

587. A mother-in-law.
A woman "Hitler."

588. A motherless lad.
Had met real loss.

589. Mountebank.
Bunko meant.

590. The Mount of Parnassus.
Oft Pan's or Muses' haunt.

591. Mourning.
O, grim nun!

592. Moustaches.
Mouth cases.

593. Multiple sclerosis.
Tissue or cells limp.

594. Must.
Stum.

595. Muttering.
Emit grunt.

596. *The Mystery of Edwin Drood.*
Food endeth my weird story.

597. Nasturtiums.
Must train us.

598. National Industrial Recovery Act.
"NIRA!" "NIRA!" ever calls to duty, action.

599. National legislators.
A long senatorial list.

600. "Nearer my God to Thee."
Hymn greeted ear too.

601. Neat tailors.
Alterations.

602. Negation.
Get a "no" in.

603. A negrophilist.
An Ethiops girl.

604. Newburyport, Massachusetts.
A town trusts such as B.P. Emery.

605. The Niagara Falls.
Ah, a large fast lin.

606. The Niagara suspension bridge.
I see it hangs up o'er grand basin.

607. Nicholas the Second, Czar of Russia.
Zealous anarchists do scorn chief.

608. A nickle slot machine.
"Kale" on it? Slim chance!

609. Night sweats.
Things waste.

610. Nilghiri nettles.
Ill sting therein.

611. The nine-word square.
Quaint wonders here.

612. Nitro-phenylenediamine.
Prominent aniline dye, eh?

613. Nomenclators.
Control names.

614. Nominate.
A mention.

615. The Norwegians.
Ages we in North.

616. Nostalgia.
Lost again.

617. No trespassing.
At "Press on" sign.

618. Nova Scotia and Prince Edward Island.
Two Canadian provinces: lands I dread!

619. The nude in art.
Nature hinted.

620. The nudist colony.
(a) No untidy clothes.
(b) No clothes; nudity.

621. The obstetrician.
Seen at birth cot, I.

622. Obstinately.
Only a bit set.

623. Ocean.
Canoe.

624. Ocean steamships.
Compass in the sea.

625. Oh to be in England, now that April's there.

Lo, Spring, hath it not robed anew the lane?

626. The old-age pension.
A design to help one.

627. *Old Curiosity Shop.*
(a) Story o' pious child.
(b) This is our old copy.

628. Old England.
Golden land.

629. Old-fashioned winter.
I folded earth in snow.

630. Old masters.
Art's models.

631. The old masters.
These mold arts.

632. The old stars and stripes.
Their spotless standard.

633. An old-time Christmas.
St. Nicholas made trim.

634. Old-time songs.
Models to sing.

635. *Oliver Twist*, by Charles Dickens.
Bold crew sins at slick thievery.

636. Oliver Wendell Holmes.
He'll do in mellow verse.

637. Omphalopsychites.
(a) Pipe holy stomachs.
(b) Mopiest holy chaps.

638. One's birthday suit.
(a) This nudity so bare.
(b) Nudity has its robe.

639. One good turn deserves another.
Do rogues endorse that? No, never!

640. One hug.
Enough?

641. Orator.
To roar.

642. An ordained minister.
I ranted, "Admire no sin."

643. Organization of the Boy Scouts.
Rah! Boast of young citizens, too.

644. Osteopath.
He pats too.

645. Ottmar Mergenthaler's typecasting machine.
Linotyper, greet that strange cam mechanism.

646. Our Alma Mater.
A true moral Ma.

647. Our beloved President McKinley.
Murder by violent sickened Pole.

648. Our Christmas carols.
Chorus stirs a clamor.

649. Our Clara.
Oracular.

650. Our destiny.
It's your end.

651. Our Father Who art in Heaven.
In woe, haven for a hurt heart.

652. Our mystic Minute Men.
Nuts in you recite
"M-M-M!"

653. The overcoat.
Cover to heat.

654. A pack of cigarettes.
Tear case to pick "fag."

655. The pair of boots.
A foot pries both.

656. A pair of patent leather shoes.
Thereat a foot-apparel shines.

657. A pair of twins.
Is twain for Pa.

658. Palindromes.
Splendor am I!

659. Palindromes and reversals.
As orders, reveal Mind's Plan.

660. Panties.
A step-in.

661. Pantomimes.
Mimes on tap.

662. Parables.
Able raps.

663. *Paradise Lost.*
A peri's sad lot.

664. *Paradise Regained.*
Dead respire again.

665. Parenthesis.
Phrase set in.

666. Parental.
(a) Prenatal.
(b) Paternal.

667. Parishioner.
I hire parson.

668. Parliament.
Partial men.

669. Parliaments.
Are an M.P. list.

670. Partisan.
Raps anti.

671. Pasquiler.
Real quips.

672. Passed by the censor.
No secret has sped by.

673. The pastries.
Pies, tarts, eh?

674. Patent applied for.
Appeal oft printed.

675. A patent medicine.
I'd menace patient.

676. The paths of glory lead but to the grave.
The poet Gray doubts that Hell forgave.

677. Patisserie.
I.e., pastries.

678. Penetrates.
Enters pate.

679. The penitential season.
Note it is a Lenten phase.

680. Penuriousness.
Pennies sour us.

681. Perambulators.
Our able tramps.

682. Perpetual motion.
I pump eternal too.

683. Pershing's American Army.
Race in, Sammy, grasp Rhine!

684. A Persian fairy.
Fair as any peri.

685. Phantasmagoria.
Rap on; I am aghast.

686. Pharisaicalness.
A precisian's lash.

687. The pharmacist.
Ah, part chemist.

688. The Pharos of Alexandria.
A fit halo adorns her apex.

689. Phonetics.
Phonic set.

690. A pickerel.
Clear pike.

691. Pinafored.
If aproned.

692. Pioneer.
Opener, I.

693. Pirates.
Sea trip.

694. Pit-a-pat.
A tip-tap.

695. Pittance.
A cent tip.

696. Playmates.
Ay, pals met.

697. Plowshare.
Helps a row.

698. Poachers.
Cop hares.

699. Pocket handkerchief.
Oft reach'd pink cheek.

700. Poet laureate.
A lute to a peer.

701. Point.
On tip.

702. Policeman.
Menial cop.

703. Police protection.
Let cop cope in riot.

704. Political leaders.
Editorial scalpel.

705. Political opponents.
Opposite in poll cant.

706. Polly wants a cracker.
Sly wan parrot, cackle.

707. Ponce de Leon's Fountain of Youth.
I.e., yon fount escaped fool on hunt.

708. Poorhouse.
O, our hopes!

709. The porcelain tower of Nanking.
Ope work of gentle art in China.

710. Porcupines.
Use pin crop.

711. Poseidon, the god of the waters.
Wight oft posed; rode on the sea.

712. Positively no admittance.
No place to visit any d— time.

713. The Postmaster General.
He's letter-post manager.

714. Postponed.
Stopped? No.

715. A Potter's Field.
Fate's dire plot.

716. The prairie schooner.
Ho! Carrieth pioneers.

717. Precaution.
I put on care.

718. Predestination.
I pertain to ends.

719. Predomination.
I'd remain on top.

720. Premeditations.
At times I ponder.

721. Presbyterian.
Best in prayer.

722. A preservative.
I ever save part.

723. President Charles de Gaulle.
He's large and ill-persecuted.

724. Presidential elections.
I see politics enter land.

725. Prestidigitation.
Presto! A digit in it.

726. The Prince of Darkness.
Arch-fiend sent pokers.

727. Procyonidae.
A coon I'd prey.

728. Produce.
Due crop.

729. The professional beauty.
(a) Fair to see, but only shape.
(b) Best shapely fair one out.
(c) Fashion's real pet, you bet.

730. The professional gambler.
Reaps the blame for losing.

731. Progressives.
G.O.P.'s revisers.

732. Prolegomenon.
One long proem.

733. A promissory note.
Payor remits soon.

734. The proof readers.
Defeat shop error.

735. The preposterous.
E'er opposes truth.

736. A prophetess.
Prates hopes.

737. The proposed Isthmian canal.
Hot Panama considers it help.

738. The prosecuting attorney.
Note he gets party in court.

739. Prosecutors.
Court posers.

740. Prosperity.
Is property.

741. Protection to American industries.
O, certain duties on certain imports.

742. The proud Stars and Stripes.
Support this standard, seer.

743. The public art galleries.
Large picture halls, I bet.

744. The pugilist.
"Pug" his title.

745. The Pullman sleeping cars.
"An upper's hell," gents
claim.

746. Punishment.
Nine thumps.

747. Purchasing.
Ring up cash.

748. The pyramids of Egypt.
Thy prim tops defy age.

749. Queer togs.
Grotesque.

750. Questioner.
One querist.

751. The radiator.
A torrid heat.

752. The railroad engineers.
Real heroes—danger in it.

753. The railroad train.
Hi! I rattle and roar.

754. The railway mail service.
It's a lively car where I am.

755. Raise.
Arise.

756. Ralph Waldo Emerson.
Person whom all read.

757. The rapscallion.
An ill cheap sort.

758. "The Raven."
(a) Hat? Never!
(b) Hant? Ever!

759. Ready-made clothes.
Create shoddy male.

760. Real estate transaction.
It's a neat sale or rent act.

761. Realistic.
(a) Clarities.
(b) It is clear.

762. The Rear-Admiral Richard
E. Byrd Expedition.
Did reach a hidden polar
extremity barrier.

763. Received payment.
Every cent paid me.

764. Recipes.
Precise.

765. The reckless automobilist.
He kills; some courts
abet it.

766. The Red, White and Blue.
Hah, we bled under it.

767. Referendum.
End free rum.

768. Reform spelling.
I'm for N.G. speller.

769. Refrigerator cars.
Great icers for a R.R.

770. Regulation.
To gain rule.

771. The religious man.
In righteous male.

772. Relinquishment.
Quits inner helm.

773. A Remington rifle.
I'm long neat firer.

774. Remuneration.
(a) Our men earn it.
(b) I am one return.

775. Renunciation.
Union I recant.

776. Repeal of the dry laws.
All "Drys" fear "Wet" hope.

777. A reprisal.
Is real rap.

778. A reprobate.
Bear a toper.

779. The Republican Party.
A public partner, they.

780. Requiescat.
Quiet acres.

781. Rescue.
Secure.

782. Resort.
Or rest.

783. Restraining.
A string rein.

784. Retraction.
Or recant it.

785. Revised edition.
Edited revision.

786. Revolution.
I love to run.

787. Revolutionary.
One rivalry out.

788. Rhinestones.
Note shiners.

789. Richard the First, Coeur de Lion.
Fierce Christian! Thou red Lord.

790. Ridiculous.
Ludicrous, I.

791. *The Rime of the Ancient Mariner*, by Coleridge.
Eerie tar chimeth metre on flying ocean bird.

792. The rings of Saturn.
O, hunt star fringes.

793. Riptides.
Spirited.

794. Roald Amundsen.
Laud'd Norseman.

795. Robert Louis Stevenson.
Our best novelist, Señor!

796. Robin Goodfellow.
Wood elf or goblin.

797. *Robinson Crusoe*, by Daniel Defoe.
Friday—one boon on be-cursed isle.

798. The Rock of Gibraltar.
Lick harbor-gate fort!

799. Roentgen's cathode rays.
A stronger eye doth scan.

800. *Roget's Thesaurus of English Words and Phrases*.
Here's fun, posers! This word-garage hands us lots.

801. The Rogues' Gallery.
(a) Leery toughs glare.
(b) All our yeggs there.

802. A rolling stone gathers no moss.
Stroller on go, amasses nothing.

803. Roosevelt's Rough Riders.
Gov. R's true hero soldiers.

804. Routine.
One rut, I.

805. The Russian Government.
Men hunt sovereign Tsar.

806. The Sacred Ibis.
He is caste bird.

807. The sadirons.
Tire hands so.

808. Saint Elmo's fire.
Is lit for seamen.

809. Saint George and the dragon.
Ha! A strong giant ended ogre.

810. Saintliness.
Least in sins.

811. Saint Nicholas.
'Las! Ain't no sich.

812. Salesladies.
Lassies deal.

813. The San Francisco Bay Area.
Chance stay, or safe in a bar.

814. Sargasso Sea.
As sea o' grass.

815. Sartre.
Rarest.

816. Satisfaction.
So fit is an act.

817. Satisfied.
Is if sated.

818. Sauciness.
Causes sin.

819. Say it with flowers.
So we flirt this way.

820. The scabies.
Base itches.

821. The scandal monger.
Can go slander them.

822. *The Scarlet Letter*, by Nathaniel Hawthorne.
Can tell thee Hester hath worn an "A" bitterly.

823. Scarlet, rose, ochre.
Sacre! Three colors!

824. The Scarpines.
Span heretics.

825. The scavenger's daughter.
Crusher gave gent's death.

826. Scheherazade, the Siren Sultana.
She read us the rich zenana tales.

827. Schoolmaster.
(a) Smote scholar.
(b) The classroom.

828. Schumann's "Traumerei."
Rare music haunts men.

829. A scoundrel.
An old curse.

830. Seance.
A scene.

831. Seclusion.
Closes us in.

832. The Secret Service of the United States.
These stout detectives ferret each sin.

833. Sedimentary.
Many see dirt.

834. Seesawing.
In wee sags.

835. Semaphore.
See arm hop.

836. Senator.
A Nestor.

837. Senator-elect Magnus Johnson.
An Uncle Josh among Nestor set.

838. Sensationalism.
Is almost insane.

839. A sentence of death.
Faces one at the end.

840. Separation.
One is apart.

841. The septuagenarian.
Near that supine age.

842. Sergei Rachmaninoff.
Finger a march so fine.

843. A set of harness.
Fastens a horse.

844. The setting sun.
Sent huge tints.

845. Shadow.
How sad.

846. Shakespeare, the immortal Bard of Avon.
Oh, this remarkable man's a favored poet.

847. Shape.
Phase.

848. Sherman's march to the sea.
The hosts came; harm nears.

849. The shoe manufacturer.
Ouch! A man's feet-hurter.

850. The shoe-shining parlors.
Throng share in polishes.

851. A shooting gallery.
I really shot a gong.

852. A shoplifter.
Has to pilfer.

853. The short-eared owls.
Shrewd late hooters.

854. Shrubbery.
Berry bush.

855. The sidereal system.
See this star medley.

856. The siege and fall of Troy.
Late foes end royal fight.

857. The siege of Verdun.
Foe sent huge drive.

858. A signal of distress.
It's S.O.S. read in flags.

859. The sign of the cross.
He's right to confess.

860. *Silas Marner.*
A miser snarl.

861. The silent majority.
Majesty in their lot.

862. A silver mine.
I've minerals.

863. Simian.
Is I man?

864. The simple annals of the poor.
One plain tale from the shops.

865. The sinapism.
This pains me.

866. Sinbad the Sailor.
This bad liar's one.

867. Sinecure.
Sure nice.

868. A sinecure.
Incur ease.

869. Sir Arthur Conan Doyle's *The Hound of the Baskervilles.*
A rather nosy Sherlock hunts bad evil hole, routs fiend.

870. A siren.
I snare.

871. Sir Walter Scott.
Last Scot writer.

872. A Sister of Charity.
Chastity, fair rose.

873. Six and three.
IX stand here.

874. Skin care.
Irks acne.

875. Slanderous.
Done as slur.

876. Slantendicular.
All is run canted.

877. The sleigh ride.
Here is delight.

878. Slipperiness.
Perils spines.

879. Slithered.
Slid there.

880. Slot machines.
Cash lost in 'em.

881. Slow reading.
A single word!

882. The smith.
Hits them.

883. The Smoky City.
Choky mist yet.

884. Snoozed.
Dozes on.

885. Society.
O, icy set.

886. Softheartedness.
Often sheds tears.

887. Soldierly.
So ye drill.

888. The soldier of fortune.
To hustle friend or foe.

889. Soldiers of the Salvation Army.
A military fold save other sons.

890. Somebody's darling.
So boy demands girl.

891. Somnipathy.
A hypnotism.

892. Sophisticated.
A chit is posted.

893. The soprano singer.
Her top noises rang.

894. Sorrowed.
Sore word.

895. South America.
So much area, it.

896. Southern California.
(a) I lose on a fruit ranch.
(b) Hot sun, or life in a car.

897. The Southern Frigid Zone.
The dirt is frozen enough.

898. Sovereignty.
Ye it governs.

899. The Spanish Armada.
Ah, Spain's death ram.

900. The Speaker of the House.
He spoke for thee, the U.S.A.

901. Special delivery stamps.
Price speeds mail vastly.

902. Spectators.
Actors' pets.

903. Spirit of the dead.
This is of departed.

904. Spiritualist seances.
A spectral issue's in it.

905. Spiritual-mindedness.
A true mind dispels sin.

906. A spittoon.
Spat in, too.

907. Spring, summer, autumn, winter.
"Time's running past," we murmur.

908. A stage whisper.
We hear its gasp.

909. Staghound.
A dog hunts.

910. Stalemate.
Lame state.

911. The Standing Army of the United States.
Guarded this nation's safety; tent them.

912. Star of Bethlehem.
(a) Halts before them.
(b) Blest the far home.

913. "The Star Spangled Banner."
Blest pennant has regard.

914. State criminals.
A miscreant list.

915. Statement.
Testament.

916. State of Arizona.
I toast a far zone.

917. State of California.
(a) Fate's fair location.
(b) Catalina rose off it.

918. State of Maryland.
Am fat oyster land.

919. The State of North Carolina.
(a) Hasten on to fair Charlotte.
(b) Tarheel an' cotton for it, Sah.

920. State prison.
(a) Pen so strait.
(b) A "stir" so pent.

921. A state reform school.
Home to foster rascal.

922. Statue of Liberty.
     A style of tribute.

923. The Statue of Liberty.
     Soft-lit beauty there.

924. Steady company.
     Nay, do set my cap.

925. Stealthy.
     At the sly.

926. "Steamer."
     Sea term.

927. Steaminess.
     Seen as mist.

928. Stenographers' handiwork.
     In shorthand workers'
page.

929. Stenographic notes.
     Phonetic so strange.

930. Stephen Girard.
     This grand peer.

931. Stereopticon.
     See torn topic.

932. A steward.
     Draws tea.

933. Sticheron.
     Rich tones.

934. A stick of chewing gum.
     Thing of magic we suck.

935. Stipend.
     Spend it.

936. Stone-deaf.
     Tones fade.

937. Strait-laced.
     A deal strict.

938. The street organ.
     Song treat there.

939. Strenuousness.
     Stuns our sense.

940. A strip-teaser.
     Attire sparse.

941. Subimago.
     So I'm a bug.

942. Submarine.
     Buries man.

943. The submarine warfare.
     Fine rare water ambush.

944. Subnormal.
     Us malborn.

945. Subordinateness.
     Set in under a boss.

946. Subterfuge.
     But refuges.

947. Subtly.
     But sly.

948. The suburbanite.
     But a "Reuben" this.

949. Suggestion.
     It eggs us on.

950. Sulfarsenite.
     Sure fine salt.

951. The Sultan's harem.
     Ah, man's lust there.

952. Summation.
     I'm amounts.

953. The summer season.
     (a) Sure, man seems hot.
     (b) See, hot sun mars me.

954. The summer vacation.
     (a) A time to charm
Venus.
     (b) I'm vacant house term.

955. Sunset on the ocean.
O, hunt scene on at sea.

956. Sunshine and shadow.
Show in sun and shade.

957. Supernaturalisms.
Unrealism traps us.

958. The Supreme Court.
Prosecute thru me.

959. Surgeon.
Go, nurse.

960. The surgeon dentist.
Sets in ground teeth.

961. Surgical instruments.
Smart curing utensils.

962. Surgical operations.
Cure ails or stop gain.

963. The surrender of General Cornwallis at Yorktown.
Courtly Washington ends all terror of keener war.

964. Surtaxes.
(a) U.S. extras.
(b) Us extras.

965. Survival of the fittest.
Tut! This life favors vet!

966. Suspended animation.
Supine man is not dead.

967. Swallowing.
All now swig.

968. Sweat.
Waste.

969. Swedish nightingale.
Sing high, sweet Linda.

970. Sweetheart.
(a) There we sat.
(b) She we treat.

971. Sweetheart days.
(a) See, we had a tryst.
(b) Dates set her way.

972. Sympathetical.
Ah, calmest pity.

973. A symphony orchestra.
So scrape thy harmony.

974. A table d'hote dinner.
An art; be hotel dined.

975. Tale-bearer.
Be a relater.

976. *Tales of a Wayside Inn.*
I'd feast away on lines.

977. A tambourine.
I mean tabour.

978. Tambourined.
I beat on drum.

979. *The Taming of the Shrew.*
Her mate won the fights.

980. *The Taming of the Shrew*, by William Shakespeare.
Kate, ye termagant wife, helps abolish her whims.

981. The Tam o' Shanter caps.
Apt Scotsman hat here.

982. Tantrums.
Must rant.

983. Tatterdemalion.
Meant old attire.

984. Tax collections.
Exact coin tolls.

985. Tearfulness.
Fears lent us.

986. Telegraph operators.
Poles gather a report.

987. A telephone girl.
Repeating "Hello."

988. A telescope.
To see place.

989. Tempestuous.
Seems put out.

990. Ten Commandments.
Can't mend most men.

991. Ten nights in a barroom.
No sober man art nigh it.

992. Tennis.
In nets.

993. Tergiversation.
(a) Is a reverting to.
(b) O, I start veering.

994. Termagant.
Target—man!

995. Termination.
Ran into time.

996. A terpsichorean.
Ah, siren to caper.

997. Tewfikose.
Sweet if O.K.

998. That settles it.
Let this attest.

999. A theater pass.
Spareth a seat.

1000. Theatrical costumes.
I am art's cute clothes.

1001. Theatrical representations.
(a) Listen! A terpsichorean treat.
(b) The entire act is personal art.

(c) Latter thespian recreations.

(d) The eternal operatic strains.

(e) Pernoctalian artistes there.

1002. Theodore Roosevelt.
(a) Hero told to oversee.
(b) He overrode loot set.

1003. Theological seminaries.
Sole aim, teach religions.

1004. Therapeutics.
Apt is the cure.

1005. Thermopylae.
Let army hope.

1006. The thirteen original colonies.
One coalition retireth English.

1007. This ear.
It hears.

1008. Thomas Carlyle.
(a) Cry shame to all.
(b) Mercy! Lash a lot.

1009. Thomas Carlyle's *Sartor Resartus.*
The story rolls rare sarcasm at us.

1010. Thomas Alva Edison, the inventor.
He lit homes, and over vast nation.

1011. Three score years and ten.
So thy career nearest end.

1012. Three sheets in the wind.
Red wines then hit these.

1013. A thunder shower.
One hard wet rush.

1014. Thunderstorm.
Thor must rend.

1015. Tied to his mother's apron-strings.
Matron is dotish: girts her pet son.

1016. Tiers etat.
Tri-estate.

1017. Time and tide wait for no man.
A fine mandate to mind, I 'trow.

1018. Time card.
I'm traced.

1019. *Timon of Athens* (Shakespeare).
Misanthrope has fate so keen.

1020. Timothy grass.
Most hay grist.

1021. The Titanic disaster.
It cast in death's rite.

1022. To be your valentine.
Yet none but a lover I.

1023. Toboggan slide.
Got on a big sled.

1024. To cast pearls before swine.
One's labor is perfect waste.

1025. To douse the glims.
Lights do seem out.

1026. To make yourself scarce.
Cue of "Scram! Katy, or else . . ."

1027. The tomb of Mausolus.
Famous but lost home.

1028. Tom Hood's *Rhymester*.
(a) Short mode to rhymes.
(b) Store o' rhythm's mode.

1029. The tonsorial artist.
(a) Starts on hair toilet.
(b) So I start in to lather.

1030. Topics of the day.
Copy of this date.

1031. The tornado.
On to dearth.

1032. Tortoise-shell butterfly.
O, it'll flutter by the roses.

1033. A tosspot.
Spot a sot.

1034. Total abstainers.
Sit not at ale bars.

1035. Touchstone.
Oh, unco test.

1036. Tourmaline.
Mineral out.

1037. Tower of London.
One old fort now.

1038. The tracheotomist.
Hi! Come test throat.

1039. Tradesmen.
Need marts.

1040. Traditor.
D— traitor.

1041. Traffic rules.
Careful first.

1042. Tragedian.
Egad! I rant.

1043. Train.
It ran.

1044. The trained nurses.
Tender hearts in us.

1045. Transatlantic voyagers.
Crony tars navigate salt.

1046. Transgressions.
As stronger sins.

1047. The transit of Venus.
It hunts Star of Even.

1048. Transportation.
Trots on in a trap.

1049. The Trans-Siberian Railroad.
Has trains ride on bare trail.

1050. The traveling salesman.
Ah, even smart at selling.

1051. Treacherous.
Ruse or cheat.

1052. The treason of Benedict Arnold.
Lo! None defend the traitor scab.

1053. *Treasure Island.*
Is sure darn tale.

1054. Tree of Knowledge of Good and Evil.
God grew food in Eden! Eve took fall.

1055. Trial balance sheets.
Able test in real cash.

1056. Tribulations.
Is but on trial.

1057. Tribute to May.
To a trim beauty.

1058. A trip around the world.
Hard to plan wider tour.

1059. The troglodytes.
They led to grots.

1060. Trolley ride.
Tired ye roll.

1061. The troubadour.
Thou outre bard.

1062. Troubles.
Blue sort.

1063. True love never runs smooth.
The storm over, rule on, Venus.

1064. Trustworthiness.
(a) Truth's sworn ties.
(b) I now stress truth.

1065. The turncoat.
Note that cur.

1066. Turn the rascals out.
Oust the tarnal curs.

1067. Twain.
In twa.

1068. *Twenty Thousand Leagues Under the Sea.*
Huge water tale stuns. End had you tense.

1069. Twinges.
We sting.

1070. The typewriter.
Write pretty, eh?

1071. Uintah.
In Utah.

1072. Ulysses Simpson Grant.
Surpassingness my lot.

1073. Unadorned.
And/or nude.

1074. Unanimity.
Am in unity.

1075. Uncertainties.
Insecure taint.

1076. Unconventionalities.
Unite in novel actions.

1077. Undertone.
Drone tune.

1078. Undiplomatic.
Mad, unpolitic.

1079. Unearthly.
Thy unreal.

1080. Unfortunate.
At no true fun.

1081. Uniformity.
I form unity.

1082. United.
In duet.

1083. United States.
(a) In te Deus stat. [God stand in thee.]
(b) Inde tute stas. [Hence thou standest safely.]
(c) A te desistunt. [They keep off from thee.]
(d) Tested as unit.

1084. United States Bond.
And 'tis U.S. debt note.

1085. The United States Bureau of Fisheries.
I raise the bass to feed us in the future.

1086. United States history.
Dates unite this story.

1087. The United States Marine Corps.
U.S. sent it to death in mere scrap.

1088. The United States of America.
(a) Attaineth its cause: freedom.
(b) That acme federation ties us.
(c) So much in a tea fee started it.
(d) O fate! Enthusiasm created it.

1089. The United States Supreme Court.
Respect us; true men that sue do it.

1090. The University of Illinois.
Illini youth strive so fine.

1091. The Unknown Soldier.
Unlisted—knew honor.

1092. Unmarried.
Unmarred, I.

1093. An unmarried woman.
A man-admirer unwon.

1094. The unmarried woman.
Worried; hunt me a man.

1095. Unmercifulness.
Cruel men in fuss.

1096. Unrighteousness.
Guess then our sin.

1097. Unshielded.
Is held nude.

1098. Unsightly.
Hints ugly.

1099. An unsolved enigma.
Nae, no man divulges.

1100. Unsubstantiated testimony.
Suits any statement in doubt.

1101. Untutoredness.
Tut! No rudeness.

1102. Upholsterers.
Restore plush.

1103. The U.S. Coast Artillery Corps.
Actually protects shore, Sir.

1104. The U.S. Library of Congress.
It's only for research bugs!

1105. The U.S. steamers Trenton, Vandalia, and Nipsic wrecked on Upolu Island by a hurricane.
Cyclone in Apia Harbor! And it tilted up and sunk three unsound American war vessels.

1106. Vacation times.
I'm not as active.

1107. Valedictorian.
Lead in a victor.

1108. Valetudinarian.
A nature invalid.

1109. The Valley of the Shadow of Death.
What have fools had to defy Lethe?

1110. The valley of unrest.
Left unsavory Lethe.

1111. Vanities.
Vain ties.

1112. Vendue-master.
Ventures made.

1113. Venetian gondoliers.
Ride in lagoon events.

1114. The Versailles Peace Conference.
Allies convene here; perfect case.

1115. Versatility.
Variety list.

1116. The veterinary surgeon.
I never hurt sore nag yet.

1117. Victoria, England's Queen.
Governs a nice quiet land.

1118. The Victor Talking Machines.
Charming voices that tinkle.

1119. Villainousness.
An evil soul's sin.

1120. Vindicate.
Act divine.

1121. Violet.
Love it.

1122. Violet, indigo, blue, green, yellow, orange, red.
Ye need love gold rainbow lure; I ignore gelt.

1123. Violets.
    (a) It's love.
    (b) I've lost.

1124. Virtue is its own reward.
    Is truer view toward sin.

1125. Virulent.
    Vile turn.

1126. Vitamines.
    Vim in eats.

1127. Vociferation.
    Strain of voice.

1128. A volcanic island.
    Land is conic lava.

1129. A volcanic mountain.
    Lava in a conic mount.

1130. The Volstead Act enforcement.
    Farce! Men covet the old'n taste.

1131. Volunteer fire departments.
    Run to divert flame ere spent.

1132. Volunteers.
    Never louts.

1133. Votes for women.
    New sort of move.

1134. The wages of sin is death.
    (a) Gee! Fate's shadow in this.
    (b) High fees owed satanist.

1135. The waiters.
    With eaters.

1136. Waitress.
    A stew, Sir?

1137. The wandering albatrosses.
    On, largest birds when at sea!

1138. War correspondents.
    Can send row reports.

1139. The war correspondents.
    To render hot scrap news.

1140. The war dance of the American Indians.
    A feather'd red man in a nice antic show.

1141. Warren Gamaliel Harding.
    Him laggard? A real winner.

1142. Washington at Valley Forge.
    (a) A few, they all go on starving.
    (b) Galling woe at frosty haven.

1143. Washington crossing the Delaware.
    (a) He saw his ragged continentals row.
    (b) A wet crew gain Hessian stronghold.

1144. The Washington Monument.
    Oh, what stunning memento.

1145. Waterspout.
    A wet sprout.

1146. The water wagons.
    What "Wets" rage on.

1147. Weather vanes.
Ah, veer at N.E.S.W.

1148. *Webster's Third New International Dictionary of the English Language,* unabridged.
When it began, this edition created one hell of a stir, 'n' "ain't" was ungrudgingly barred!

1149. *Webster's Unabridged Dictionary.*
Grand edition used by ABC writers.

1150. A wedding ceremony.
Ye ceded woman ring.

1151. Weird nightmares.
Thing we dream, Sir.

1152. Western Union.
No wire unsent.

1153. What in the world!
Halt with wonder.

1154. A whirling dervish.
Has whirring devil.

1155. The white clover blossom.
Loveth rich sweet blooms.

1156. White feather.
Fear with thee.

1157. Whithersoever.
Oh, wherever 'tis.

1158. The widow's mite.
Two white dimes.

1159. The widow's weeds.
We didst shew woe.

1160. Wild goose chase.
Chose wide goals.

1161. Wild oats.
Lad sow it.

1162. William Ewart Gladstone.
(a) Wilt tear down *all* images?
(b) Wild agitator means well.
(c) Will mislead a great town.
(d) We want a mild legislator.
(e) Wit so great will lead men.
(f) A man to wield great wills.
(g) Go, administrate law well.
(h) At will, great wise old man.

1163. William Gaynor.
A willing mayor.

1164. William Howard Taft.
A word with all—I'm fat.

1165. William J. Bryan.
(a) Brainy jaw-mill.
(b) Will bray in jam.

1166. William Penn's treaty with the Indians.
Wise Lennis part with the land in amity.

1167. William Shakespeare.
(a) We all make his praise.
(b) I ask me, has Will a peer.

1168. Women.
Won me.

1169. The zoological gardens.
Oh, gaze into droll cages!

Palindromic Sentences

For the following list of palindromic sentences I am chiefly indebted to Leigh Mercer, who supplied me with the vast majority of them. In reply to my questions concerning their authorship, he has written "The question is difficult—many were started by A and improved by B." While this collection is without a doubt the work of many hands, it is also virtually certain that a large proportion of them are the creations of Leigh Mercer himself—although he has given no indication at all in the lists he sent me which of the sentences are his own. At least this much can be said: Mr. Mercer is well-known to have composed the "Straw-warts," the "Doom, royal panic," and the superb "Erasmus" palindromes; yet he may very well have also composed a hundred or more of those that remain. Some, of course, can be definitely attributed to other authors: the beautiful "Rowena" palindrome ("A new order began . . .") is the work of Dmitri A. Borgmann, of Oak Park, Illinois; and the "mad as a hatter" palindrome was constructed by the late Hercules McPherrin, of Denver, Colorado. But who is responsible for the amazing one on goddesses? I have not been able to find out. Anyone who tries to track these things down may run into surprises. James Michie, of London, published the "Doc, note" palindrome in the London publication, the *New Statesman* (May 5, 1967). But when I wrote to him, he wrote back, "I did not make it up. It was told to me by a mathematician in 1944 who did not make it up either." And so it goes. In any case, the reader will find in these sentences a large part of the thematic material which the language provides—material which will, eventually, and in the fullness of time, be evolved into larger and more intricate shapes at the touch of innumerable other talents.

PALINDROMIC SENTENCES

Able was I ere I saw Elba.

Ah, Aristides opposed it, sir, aha!

Ah, Satan sees Natasha.

All erotic, I lose my lyme solicitor, Ella.

Al lets Della call Ed, Stella.

Analytic Paget saw an inn in a waste-gap city, Lana.

A new order began, a more Roman age bred Rowena.

Anne, I stay a day at Sienna.

Anne, I vote more cars race Rome-to-Vienna.

Arden saw I was Nedra.

Are we not drawn onwards, we Jews, drawn onward to new era?

Are we not, Rae, near to new era?

A rod, not a bar, a baton, Dora.

Ban campus motto, "Bottoms up, MacNab."

Bob: "Did Anna peep?" Anna: "Did Bob?"

Bog dirt up a sidetrack carted is a putrid gob.

Damosel, a poem? A carol? Or a cameo pale? (So mad!)

Deer frisk, sir, freed.

Degas, are we not drawn onward, we freer few, drawn onward to
    new eras aged?

"Degenerate Moslem, a cad!" Eva saved a camel so Meta reneged.

Delia and Edna ailed.

Delia sailed as sad Elias ailed.

Delia, here we nine were hailed.

Delia sailed, Eva waved, Elias ailed.

Delia's debonair dahlias, poor, drop or droop. Sail, Hadrian; Obed
    sailed.

Deliver, Eva, him I have reviled.

"Deliver desserts," demanded Nemesis, "emended, named, stressed,
    reviled."

Dennis, no misfit can act if Simon sinned.

Deny me not; atone, my Ned.

Desserts I desire not, so long no lost one rise distressed.

Did Dean aid Diana? Ed did.

Did Hannah say as Hannah did?

Di, did I as I said I did?

Did Ione take Kate? No, I did.

Did I do, O God, did I as I *said* I'd do? Good, I did!

Did I draw Della too tall, Edward? I did?

Doc, note, I dissent. A fast never prevents a fatness. I diet on cod.

Dog as a devil deified, lived as a god.

Do Good's deeds live on? No, Evil's deeds do, O God.

"Do nine men interpret?" "Nine men," I nod.

Do not start at rats to nod.

Doom an evil deed, liven a mood.

Doom, royal panic, I mimic in a play or mood.

Dora tendered net, a rod.

Drab as a fool, as aloof as a bard.

Drab Reg, no longer bard.

Draw—aye, no melody—dole-money award.

Draw no dray a yard onward.

Draw, O Caesar, erase a coward.

Draw, O coward!

Draw pupil's pup's lip upward.

Egad, a base life defiles a bad age.

Egad, a base tone denotes a bad age.

Egad! Loretta has Adams as mad as a hatter. Old age!

Emil asleep, Allen yodelled "Oy." Nella peels a lime.

Emil, asleep, Hannah peels a lime.

Enid and Edna dine.

Ere hypocrisies or poses are in, my hymn I erase. So prose I, sir,
    copy here.

Euston saw I was not Sue.

Euston sees not Sue.

Eva, can I pose as Aesop in a cave?

Eva, can I stab bats in a cave?

Evade me, Dave.

Eve damned Eden, mad Eve.

Eve saw diamond, erred, no maid was Eve.

Evil is a name of a foeman, as I live.

Gate-man sees name, garage-man sees name-tag.

God, a red nugget! A fat egg under a dog!

Goddesses so pay a possessed dog.

"Go, droop aloof," sides reversed, is "fool a poor dog."

Golf? No, sir, prefer prison-flog.

Ha! I rush to my lion oily moths, Uriah!

Harass selfless Sarah!

Harass sensuousness, Sarah.

Ha! Robed Selim smiles, Deborah!

He lived as a devil, eh?

Hell! A spacecraft farce caps all, eh?

Help Max, Enid—in example "H."

Here so long? No loser, eh?

In airy Sahara's level, Sarah, a Syrian, I.

In a regal age ran I.

I made border bard's drowsy swords; drab, red-robed am I.

I maim nine men in Saginaw; wan, I gas nine men in Miami.

I maim nine more hero-men in Miami.

I, man, am regal; a German am I.

I, Marian, I too fall; a foot-in-air am I.

I moan, "Live on, O evil Naomi!"

I roamed under it as a tired, nude Maori.

I saw desserts; I'd no lemons, alas no melon. Distressed was I.

I saw thee, madame, eh? 'Twas I.

I told Edna how to get a mate: "Go two-handed." Loti.

"Knight, I ask nary rank," saith gink.

Ladle histolytic city lots I held, Al.

Lapp, Mac? No, sir, prison-camp pal.

Lay a wallaby baby ball away, Al.

Lepers repel.

Lew, Otto has a hot towel.

Live dirt up a sidetrack carted is a putrid evil.

Live not on evil.

Live not on evil deed, live not on evil.

Live not on evil, madam, live not on evil.

Live on, *Time*; emit no evil.

Live was I ere I saw Evil.

Madame, not one man is selfless; I name not one, Madam.

Madam, I'm Adam.

Madam, in Eden I'm—Adam.

Ma is a nun, as I am.

Ma is as selfless as I am.

"Ma," Jerome raps pot top, "spare more jam!"

Marge let a moody baby doom a telegram.

Marge lets Norah see Sharon's telegram.

Marge, lets "went." I await news telegram.

Max, I stay away at six A.M.

May a moody baby doom a yam?

Milestones? Oh, 'twas I saw those, not Selim.

Mirth, sir, a gay asset? No, don't essay a garish trim.

Moorgate got nine men in to get a groom.

Moors dine, nip—in Enid's room.

Mother at song no star, eh Tom?

Mother Eve's noose we soon sever, eh, Tom?

Must sell at tallest sum.

Name I—Major-General Clare—negro Jamie Man.

Naomi, did I moan?

Ned, go gag Ogden.

Ned, I am a maiden.

Nella, demand a lad named Allen.

Nella risks all: "I will ask Sir Allen."

Nella's simple hymn: "I attain my help, Miss Allen."

Nella won't set a test now, Allen.

Nemo, we revere women.

Never a foot too far, even.

Niagara, O roar again!

No benison, no sin, Ebon.

No Dot nor Ottawa "legal age" law at Toronto, Don.

Noel, did I not rub Burton? I did, Leon.

Noel, lets egg Estelle on.

Noel saw I was Leon.

Noel sees Leon. / Leon sees Noel. [Two palindromes.]

No evil Shahs live on.

No, Hal, I led Delilah on.

No ham came, sir, now siege is won. Rise, MacMahon.

No, I save on final perusal, a sure plan if no evasion.

No, is Ivy's order a red rosy vision?

No, it can assess an action.

No, it's a bar of gold, a bad log for a bastion.

No, it is open on one position.

No, it is opposed; Art sees Trade's opposition.

No, it is opposition.

No, it never propagates if I set a "gap" or prevention.

No lemons, no melon.

No Misses ordered roses, Simon.

No mists or frost, Simon.

Nomists reign at Tangier, St. Simon.

Nora, alert, saws goldenrod-adorned logs, wastrel Aaron!

Norah's foes order red rose of Sharon.

"Norah's moods," Naomi moans, "doom Sharon."

Nor I, fool, ah no! We won halo—of iron.

Nor I nor Emma had level'd a hammer on iron.

Norma is as selfless as I am, Ron.

No, set a maple here, help a mate, son.

"Not for Cecil?" asks Alice Crofton.

Not I, no hotel, cycle to Honiton.

"Not New York," Roy went on.

"Novrad," sides reversed, is "Darvon."

No waste, grab a bar, get saw on.

"Now dine," said I as Enid won.

Now do I repay a period won.

Now do I report "Sea Moth" to Maestro, period? Won.

Now ere we nine were held idle here, we nine were won.

Now Eve, we're here, we've won.

Now Ned, I am a maiden nun; Ned, I am a maiden won.

Now, Ned, I am a maiden won.

No word, no bond, row on.

Now saw ye no mosses or foam, or aroma of roses. So money was won.

Now, sir, a war is won! / A war at Tarawa! [Two palindromes.]

Nurse, save rare vases, run! / A dog! A panic in a pagoda! [Two palindromes.]

Nurse, I spy gypsies, run!

Nurse's onset abates, noses run.

O gnats, tango!

Oh who was it I saw, oh who?

On tub, Edward imitated a cadet; a timid raw debut, no?

O render gnostic illicit song, red Nero.

Paget saw an inn in a waste gap.

Pa's a sap.

Pat and Edna tap.

Peel's lager on red rum did murder no regal sleep.

"Pooh," smiles Eva, "have Selim's hoop."

Poor Dan is in a droop.

Pull a bat! I held a ladle, hit a ball up.

Pull up, Eva, we're here, wave, pull up.

Pull up if I pull up. / Too hot to hoot. [Two palindromes.]

Pusillanimity obsesses Boy Tim in "All Is Up."

Puss, a legacy! Rat in a snug, unsanitary cage, lass, up!

"Rats gnash teeth," sang Star.

Rats live on no evil star.

Red now on level—no wonder.

Red roses run no risk, sir, on nurses order.

Red? Rum, eh? 'Twas I saw the murder.

Refasten Gipsy's pig-net safer.

Regard a mere mad rager.

Reg, no lone car won, now race no longer.

Red root put up to order.

Remit Rome cargo to go to Grace Mortimer.

Repel evil as a live leper.

Resume so pacific a pose, muser.

Retracting, I sign it, Carter.

Revenge my baby, Meg? Never!

Revered now I live on. O did I do no evil, I wonder ever?

"Reviled did I live," said I, "as evil I did deliver."

"Revolt, love!" raved Eva. "Revolt, lover!"

Revolt on Yale, Democrats edit "Noon-Tide Star." Come, delay not, lover.

Rise, morning is red, no wonder-sign in Rome, Sir.

Rise to vote, Sir. / Name now one man. [Two palindromes.]

Ron, Eton mistress asserts I'm no tenor.

Roy Ames, I was a wise mayor.

Roy, am I mayor?

Sail on, game vassal! Lacy callas save magnolias!

Saladin enrobes a baroness, Señora, base-born Enid, alas.

Salisbury moor, sir, is roomy. Rub Silas.

"Sal is not in?" Ruth asks. "Ah, turn it on, Silas."

See few owe fees.

See, slave, I demonstrate yet arts no medieval sees.

Selim's tired, no wonder, it's miles.

Semite, be sure! Damn a man-made ruse betimes.

Set a broom on no moor, Bates.

Sh! Tom sees moths.

Sir, I demand, I am a maid named Iris.

Sir, I'm Iris.

Sir, I soon saw Bob was no Osiris.

"Sirrah! Deliver deified desserts *detartrated*!" stressed deified,
    reviled Harris.

Sis, Sargasso moss a grass is.

Sit on a potato pan, Otis.

Si, we'll let Dad tell Lewis.

Six at party, no pony-trap, taxis. / 'Tis Ivan on a visit. [Two palin-
    dromes.]

"Slang is not suet, is it?" Euston signals.

Slap-dab set-up, Mistress Ann asserts, imputes bad pals.

Snug Satraps eye Sparta's guns.

"So I darn on," a Canon radios.

So may Apollo pay Amos.

So may get Arts award. Draw a strategy, Amos.

So may Obadiah aid a boy, Amos.

So may Obadiah, even in Nineveh, aid a boy, Amos.

Some men interpret nine memos.

So remain a mere man. I am Eros.

Sore was I ere I saw Eros.

Star? Come, Donna Melba, I'm an amiable man—no Democrats!

Stella won no wallets.

St. Eloi, venin saved a mad Eva's nine violets.

Stephen, my hat! Ah, what a hymn, eh, pets?

Step on hose-pipes? Oh no, pets.

Step on no pets!

Stop! Murder us not tonsured rumpots!

"Stop!" nine myriad murmur. "Put up rum, *rum*, dairymen, in
    pots."

Stop, Syrian, I see bees in airy spots.

Stop, Syrian, I start at rats in airy spots.

St. Simon sees no mists.

Straw? No, too stupid a fad. I put soot on warts.

Sue, dice, do, to decide us.

"Sue," Tom smiles, "Selim smote us."

"Suit no regrets." A motto, Master Gerontius.

Sums are not set as a test on Erasmus.

Telegram, Margelet!

Ten animals I slam in a net.

Ten dip a rapid net.

Tenet C is a basis, a basic tenet.

Tennis set won now Tess in net.

Ten? No bass orchestra tarts, eh? Cross a bonnet!

Tense, I snap Sharon roses, or Norah's pansies net.

Tessa's in Italy, Latin is asset.

Tide-net safe, soon, Allin. A manilla noose fastened it.

To nets, ah, no, son, haste not.

Too bad, I hid a boot.

Too far away, no mere clay or royal ceremony, a war afoot.

Too far, Edna, we wander afoot.

Top step—Sara's pet spot.

Top step's pup's pet spot.

Tracy, no panic in a pony-cart.

Trade ye no mere moneyed art.

Trap a rat! Stare, piper, at Star apart.

War-distended nets I draw.

"Warden in a Cap," Mac's pup scamp, a canine draw.

Ward nurses run "draw."

Was it a rat I saw? / No, miss, it is Simon. [Two palindromes.]

Was it felt? I had a hit left, I saw.

Was raw tap ale not a reviver at one lap at Warsaw?

We'll let Dad tell Lew.

We seven, Eve, sew.

Wonders in Italy, Latin is "Red" now.

Won race, so loth to lose car now.

Won't I repaper? Repaper it now.

Won't lovers revolt now?

Yawn a more Roman way.

Yes, Mark, cable to hotel, "Back Ramsey."

Yes, Syd, Owen saved Eva's new Odyssey.

Yo! Bottoms up, U.S. Motto, boy!

Zeus was deified, saw Suez.

An Informal Note
on a Variety of Things

Circular reversals are a curious type of word which, when written clockwise in a circle, may be read counter-clockwise—starting at a suitable point—to yield another word, phrase, or sentence. Some examples:

Dmitri	I'm dirt.
Synopsis	Pony's sis.
Ungarbed	Brag, nude!
Playmate	Al, pet Amy.
Premature	Peru-tamer!
Mayonnaise	I annoy Ames.
Betasyamine	I may sate Ben.

"Peru-tamer" is, of course, a bold sobriquet for Francisco Pizarro. "Betasyamine" is a registered trade-name for a medicine which was developed for the treatment of muscle-wasting diseases, but which has, unfortunately, been out of production since 1955.

Professor Yuen Ren Chao (Department of Oriental Languages, University of California, Berkeley) is a man who can talk and sing backwards. I quote from a letter from Professor Chao:

> My interest in reversed speech came from the analysis of sound seg-ments in various languages, especially in English, in which many of the phonemes are actually phonetically complex and the phonetic complexity comes out strikingly because of the irreversibility. That is why it is so hard to find genuine phonetic palindromes that are phonographically reversible.

In the realm of the phonographically reversible there are many surprises. Phonetic palindromes do not, as a rule, look a bit like graphic palindromes. Professor Chao has provided the following examples of:

1. *Phonetically palindromic words:* shush, church, George, sauce, cease, babe, known.
2. *Phonetically reversible word pairs:* tea—eat; star—arts; but—tub; nil—loin (not lin).
3. *Sentences which are phonetic palindromes:*

    Madam, I am Adam.

    Did you say we are dead, Bob? Ahaha, Bob, dead, are you? Yes, we did.*

Returning to graphic palindromes, we stop for a brief interval at the studio of a palindromist who resides in Woodstock, New York.

Reign at Suez, Zeus! Tangier!

[Olympus has become rather stodgy over the years—(Probably advice from Venus, or Europa, or somebody . . .)]

Allah, lave Valhalla!

[A pious Moslem speaks.]

Llul sagas lull.

[Ramon Llul was a medieval philosopher—I don't think he is much read nowadays, outside of Mallorca.]

Animal loots foliated detail of stool lamina.

Espagnola solos along apse.

[She's always alone. Why?]

Red robber gazes not on S.E. Zagreb border.

. . . Ever,

Yr. Eve.

Draught nine men in th' guard.

Yacht notes radar set on th' cay.

¡O cita Mora! Aromatico!

[I roll my cigarets and use "Bambu" papers which come from Spain. The word "Aromatico" occurs on the package, and I looked at it a lot of years before seeing the possibilities of the word.]

* The following may be helpful in comprehending phonetic palindromes. Note the words WE and YOU. WE is really the diphthong OO-EE in which the OO is sounded rather briefly and the EE is more sustained; and YOU is in fact the reverse diphthong EE-OO, except that in this case it is the EE that is brief and the OO more sustained. Slight liberties must be taken with pronunciation of some words to make them phonographically reversible.—H.W.B.

Young Sten nets gnu! Oy!
[When young Sten was Bar-Mitzvahed, Sten Sr. took him on Safari, as
a present; during the course of which Mrs. Sten received this jubilant
telegram.]

—John McClellan

McClellan's variant spelling of "cigarettes" in his note to his
beautiful Spanish palindrome has reminded me of a fascinating story
told to me by J. A. Lindon, whose letter I quote:

> Did I ever tell you that an old friend of mine, a heavy smoker who died
> of lung cancer, once dreamed the words
>
> > The tragic
> > magic
> > of setteragic.
>
> Curious, eh? Obviously his mind was trying to get it through to him,
> disguising the message so as to make it palatable.

Four Occasional
Palindromic Poets

Without a doubt there will be many readers of this book who would
like to have an opportunity to make their own comparative studies
of the ways in which different poets conceive and execute the
palindromic poem. It is a major part of my purpose to provide for
such readers what few artistic examples are known to me. As is not
the case with other—especially twentieth-century—poetry, in
logological poetry (a literary genus embracing a diversity of
fascinating species of which the palindrome is, in fact, but one) the
demands of form are so great that it becomes relatively easy for the
reader to separate the genuine artist, however humble his endow-
ment, from the humbug. In my judgment, the six palindromic
poems given below merit preservation.

Sutra Poems Pass

> Sutra poems pass, alas: O resign.
> O stratagem! In, I'm in.
> I'm won!
> Deified!
> Now mini-mini mega-tart song
> Is "Eros, alas, saps me."
> O part us.

—John Wardroper

Puma, Puma!

Puma, puma! Iris won!
  (Mural art)
Puck-cap I was—lived a Don
  (No mural, mural art)

Nor I, Pater. If, as no slender stem, meek,
    I lose—beware dew!
O vassal, can I wonder? Red is a star;
    Evil partner—wallahs deified.
Shall a wren trap live rats?—As I'd erred now
    In a class-avowed era?
We be so like emmets. . . .
    Red Nelson's afire; tap iron!
Tralarum, larum. On nod, a Devil saw I—
    Pack cup!
Tralarum! Now, sir, I am up—
    Am up.

—Hubert Phillips

REPORT GIVEN TO THE LADY CHAIRMAN OF A MUTUAL DEIFICATION ASSOCIATION

Anna, deified, sees deified Noel and Edna, Madam;
Nella, deified, sees deified Miles and Edna, Madam;
Dot, deified, sees deified Tod, Madam, and Edna;
Selim, deified, sees deified Allen, Madam, and Edna;
Leon, deified, sees deified Anna.

—Leigh Mercer and Dmitri Borgmann

MOOD'S MODE

Mood's mode!
Pallas, I won!
(Diaper pane, sold entire.)
Melt till ever sere, hide it.
Drown a more vile note;
(Tar of rennet.)
Ah, trowel, baton, eras ago.
The reward? A "nisi." Two nag.

Otary tastes putrid, yam was green.
Odes up and on; stare we.
Rots nod. Nap used one-erg saw.
(May dirt upset satyr?)

A toga now; 'tis in a drawer, eh?
Togas are notable.
(Worth a tenner for Até.)
Tone liver. O Man, word-tied I.

Here's revel!
Little merit, Ned? Lose, Nap?
Repaid now is all apedom's doom.

—*Hubert Phillips*

FOUR PALINDROMES OF THE APOCALYPSE

An era, midst its dim arena
Elapses pale.
No, in uneven union
Liars, alas, rail.

—*Leigh Mercer*

I have suggested elsewhere in these pages that the palindromically potent elements of our language will probably be evolved into ever more elaborate and astonishing forms as time goes on. The Principle of Evolution is ubiquitous, and Evolution is the Great Experimenter. It is interesting to see how the mind of one palindromist interacts with the product of the mind of another. Below, the reader may see how Dmitri Borgmann, being both attracted and dissatisfied by a particular palindromic couplet (shown first), has re-envisioned it.

Anadem—ah! Saturnism! O sob, nude baroness—Apostolate Roma.
Amoret, a lot so passé! Nor abed unbosom sin—rut ashamed, Ana.

—*from " O Tongue in Cheek"*

Deliver Evil Norah's diadem, ah, Saturnism!
O sob, nude baroness, apropos a sopor passé!
Nor, abed, unbosom sin:
Rut ashamed, aid Sharon live reviled!

—*Dmitri A. Borgmann*

Selected Palindromic Poems
of Graham Reynolds

Graham Reynolds is one of the very few poets in the English-speaking
world who has long cultivated the palindromic poem, wooed it, and
found it beautiful. Comparison of his work with that of J. A. Lindon,
Hubert Phillips, and others makes it evident that the difficulties of
the form are not a bar to the development of widely different styles.

SHIPWRECK

Ebb be.
Sloops' sleek keels.
Deeps speed.
Dirge, gride;
Race, fast salt,
A deluge guled.
Oh surf, rush,
O, gibe
Big swash saws;
Reel, leer.
Yaw. A raft.
Far eve,
Tar at dusk,
Cord, lock,
Rack, cark,
Cold rock,
Sud,
Tar at eve,
Raft far away.
Reel, leer,

Swash saws,
Gibe big,
Oh, surf, rush
O deluge guled.
At last safe.
Care, dirge, grid.
Deeps speed,
Sleek keels' spools:
Ebb be.

DRINKING SONG

Avid as a diva
O gin, on, on I go;
   Martini in it ram,
      Gorge grog,
   Bib, bib,
   Toss, sot,
      Tope lager
   Gulp tub, Burton
Retsina

Canister not rub,
   But plug.
Regale pot;
   Toss, sot
Bib, bib,
Gorge grog,
   Martini in it ram
O gin, on, on I go
   Avid as a diva.

HYMN TO THE MOON

      Luna, nul one,
      Moon, nemo,
Drown word.
   In mutual autumn
   I go;
Feel fog rob all life;
   Fill labor

Go, flee fog
  In mutual autumn
    I drown
Word; omen; no omen.
O, Luna, nul.

Valse Slav

Valse slav.
Fiery lyre if
  Music I sum,
    Romeo poem
      Or rose, yes,
    Or drowsy Pepys word.
    Rose, yes,
  Or Romeo poem,
Or music I sum.
  Fiery lyre if
    Valse slav.

O Gnat

O gnat,
  Broth
  Girl,
Lewder castanet
  Tap patten
At sacred well;
  Right orb,
    Tango.

Pall
At seven, O,
  For I dance.
  Be, rebec,
Nadir of one
  Vestal lap

O gnat,
  Broth
  Girl,
Lewder castanet

Tap patten
At sacred well;
Right orb,
Tango.

Rue Viveur

Rue Viveur
Smirk, loyal, a yolk rims
Moody doom,
Seen knees,
Tissues use us.
Sit, swap paws,
Sleeps.
Sup as soft Foss, a pussy,
A stirrup,
Purr "its at serene rest, luxe."
Exult, cat
No connoisseur rues Sion,
No contact.
Luxe, exult,
Serene rest,
A stirrup,
Purr.
It says
"Sup as soft Foss, a puss."
Peels, swap paws,
Tissues use us.
Sit, seen knees,
Moody doom;
Smirk, loyal.
A yolk rims
Rue Viveur.

Sassettas at Tessa's

Sassettas at Tessa's
Tube, glib bilge,
Riot repertoire,
Portfolio,
Slob my symbols.

Sail on, game magnolias,
To rococo rot,
Sail on, game magnolias.

Slob my symbols,
Oil of trope,
Riot repertoire,
Glib bilge, but
Sassettas at Tessa's.

A Selection from
the Palindromic Work of
J. A. Lindon

"Nod, Nila Jo, to J. A. Lindon!"

Just as in vaudeville it was always the headliner who closed the show, I likewise have reserved the last spot in this book for Lindon, who ends it not with a whimper but a bang. His would be a hard act to follow.

How pleasant to know Mr. Lindon, the gifted innovator from whose pen hundreds of palindromes flow; the creator and curator of one of the most engaging galleries of surrealistic art-objects ever conjured up by the literary imagination. In the galaxy of several hundred sentences below, plus a constellation of poems and a skit, J. A. Lindon has blazed so many fascinating new trails through the tangled palindromic possibilities of our language, that he can hardly hope to escape the accolade of Major Muse of the English Palindrome.

Nine of the (letter-unit) palindromic poems have been previously published in *Word Ways*, Vol. II, No. 1, and the skit in Vol. III, No. 4. "As I Was Passing Near the Jail" first appeared in Lindon's article, "PD Stands for Palindromes," in a London publication, *Competitors' Journal*, for May 7, 1955. "Doppelgänger" was published in an earlier version in Dmitri Borgmann's *Beyond Language* (Scribner's, 1967). Both were republished in Martin Gardner's Mathematical Games department in the August, 1970, *Scientific American*.

PALINDROMIC SENTENCES (LETTER-UNIT)

All erotic, I lose lame female solicitor Ella.
A long nip . . . Path sin? If I nap, my tympani finish tapping, Nola.

"An error—rim not on mirror, Rena." / "Risen—oh, sir!—I saw mirror-rim was Irish one, sir." [Two PDs.]

Birch-supple, his path a murk, Nkrumah taps . . . I help push crib. [*A deposed dictator going on foot into exile and taking his heir with him. Later, I regret to say, it was:*] Huge knife, ebony baby—no beef in keg, uh? / No sign if in. Kwame, babe maw-knifing is on! [Two additional PDs.]

Bishop made lame female damp? Oh, Sib!

Cigar? Toss it in a can, it is so tragic. / But sad Eva saved a stub. [Two PDs.]

Cino taximen in tavern, Rev., at nine mix a tonic.

Cite opera? We fail, Eli. A few are poetic.

Daft, I meet Señorita Edna, gorge grog and eat iron, esteem it fad.

Dairyman, ample horde pets attack, limelit. Risk, sir, tile-milk, cattaste . . . Pedro, help, man! A myriad!

Deb—a deb or Nellie (dame made ill)—enrobed abed.

Deirdre wets altar of St. Simon's—no mists, for at last ewer dried.

"Dens? Do casinos reward? Mine don't. Ned, I've still (it's evident) no denim drawers on," Isa cods Ned.

Dian, I am reviled, I turn, I dump Martin Gardner, I rend rag 'n' I tramp mud in rut, I deliver main aid. [From *How I Won the War.*]

"Di,"—as I slap—"pay no HP, my symphony appals," I said.

"Di, as Ned Alec I don't sin. I play oboe mortal flat," Romeo-boy alpinist (no dice laden) said.

Did I fish? Tim's rod or Smith's if I did.

Did I slam in a lab in N.A. cannibal animals? I did.

Did I strap red nude, red rump, also slap murdered underparts? I did.

Dim Rodney repardoned ungarbed deb, rag-nude, no drapery, end or mid!

"Drat such cod!" "Rum, sir?" ("I'm orf!") Marcel: "Liver, grisette?" "Lemonade? Cider? Free beer, Fred—iced?" "An omelette, Sir Greville? Cram!" From Iris Murdoch: "Custard?" [*Literary luncheon!*]

Eh, wash crimson? Wondered a General—a renegade, Red now, no smirch saw he.

Ellen, all I've noted: a cadet, one villanelle.

Eloped a General (a gal!), a renegade Pole.

Emir, Cadet Tim, dampening Nora's sarong, nine p.m., admitted a crime.

Er ... I fondle her as late petals are held—no fire.

Even I saw Edith Nesbit on tub, but not Ibsen (H.)—tide was in, Eve.

Fist is not silk, sir, if I risk Liston's. It's *if*—

Gert, I saw Ron avoid a radio-van—or was it Reg?

He'd no pot? Reg, Nan, Irene drag gardener in anger to pond, eh?

He peels ... "It's eleven. Rut's turn, Eve. Lest I sleep, eh?"

He's done no B! Mortal lull! A trombone nods, eh?

He wondered: Is no colossal eel as solo considered now, eh?

I'm Agnes, nineteen, I'm axed examinee ten in S.E. Ngami.

In a chair use many names, Uriah. —Can I?

I, Nora, came most egotistic—it's I—to get some macaroni.

I pot coyotes. I won't open fire, sir, at a riser if N.E. Pot nowise toy octopi.

I saw Rosa with Giles Rowan in war bed—under it! Ere we retired (nude brawn!) in a worse light I was, or was I?

I saw Rosa with Gillian's niece, in snail-light I was, or was I?

Liverish, sat nail-pared nude (Kansas) naked under a pliant ash, sir—evil!

"Massey, has Simone got an aspirin?" I rip *Sanatogen* ... "O Miss ..." "Ah, yes, Sam."

Man, Eve let an idiot—a retromastoid idiot, Sam, or teratoid—in at eleven A.M.

"Miry rim! So many daffodils," Delia wailed, "slid off a dynamo's miry rim!"

Miserable bad asset, ample hypocrisy! As I say, sir, copy helpmates sad Abel, bare Sim. / Lor! Reno's reward went up and Edna put new drawers on, Errol. [*Increased alimony, perhaps!*] [Two PDs.]

Mood severe—venom! Music I summon, ever Eve's doom.

Murder O'Dally—eh?—tenor-drone. They'll adore drum!

Ned, ay, asinine Daniel did idle in a den—in, I say, a *den*.

Nembutal? Life's reverse! Fill a tub, men!

New loose robes—oh, those!—bore so Olwen.

New lower cadets row, nine men in worsted, a *crew*, Olwen!

No dial? Fine music is U, men, if laid on.

"No drone to trio." (Memoir to tenor Don.)

Nola departs, eh? Cross. I miss orchestra, pedal on ...

Nola's. Midst sin I play sonatas at a nosy alpinist's dim salon.

Noose-born Edna, push table to hotel bath, sup and enrobe soon.

No ostracised art for Eliot, a toiler of trades, I cart soon.

North Girton sign, or "Wrong is not Right," Ron.

No; Sam—as I told a bad lot—is a mason.

No spin, pals. As I see Sara snore, dips a spider on Sara, sees Isa's lap, nips on.

"No, tip alcohol." I medicate Gert in sulphur (uh?) plus nitre . . . "Get acid, Emil—oho, clap it on!" [*Poor Gert!*]

Now slash! Superb—as a sabre-push! Sal's won!

Nurse! Major-General! (*Faded a flare*) Negro James!—RUN!

"Nurses run!" says sick Cissy as nurses run.

O dire Cremona! I prefer piano, Mercer, I do! [*Actually Mercer plays only the shoehorn, the mathematical symbols and the conundrum!*]

On hay not to nod, I hope? Elsie (my sword-mistress) asserts I'm drowsy—*me, I sleep!* Oh, I do not, Tony ah, no!

Pam's Ira passes, so, Pip, I possess a Paris map.

Pilfer a ramose broom, a moor-besom, a rare flip.

Pun: I pay a pixy no onyx, I pay a pin-up! [*Literally a pun.*]

Put Felix, if fuss arises or arose, sir (as suffix I left) up.

"Refasten net safer." / "Net safe. Rotten net to refasten." / Nets aft now. We fasten nets. A few won't fasten. [Three PDs.]

Report paracetamol is not in unit on silo, mate. Car apt.—ROPER.

Revel. Carts, eh, cross? I hiss. Orchestra clever.

"Rise! Take nine, divide nine, Kate." "Sir?"

"Risk nip a rose." Karl rakes . . . "Or a pink, sir." / Turn! I note severe Karl, Eve—level-raker, Eve—set on in rut. [*Probably his master disapproved of his giving away the flowers!*] [Two PDs.]

Risk? No! Can one melt negroes on warm raw nose or gentlemen on a conk, sir?

Satan, O Satan, ere seven, my hero (MEMO: Sin I some more), hymn Eve—serenata, sonatas . . .

Set on wold, lose—oh!—cello, Rhoda, so sad! Oh, roll echoes, old low notes!

Sex, Rex? Nil. Ever I revel in *Xerxes*! [*So saith the bookworm.*]

Sh, Rhona! I play organ, nag royal piano (HRH's).

Spare Dartmoor's Sal can in a classroom trade raps.

Spidery Gyre pardoned—a mermaid! I am remodelled, O mermaid, I am remade. No-drapery gyre . . . Dips.

Stored under strata, torsos rot, a tart's (red, nude) rots.

T. Eliot, *animé*, opens—eyes N.E.—poem in a toilet.

'Tis sent! I wed a mermaid—airy, mad, I'm amid a myriad, I am remade, witness it!

"'Tis Sim's idyll—a breviary, Myra!" I verbally dismiss it.

To Pa Ettie ceded *urn*? Rude deceit—*teapot*!

Top deb, an Osiris girl—lord, droll rig, sir!—is on a bed-pot.

Trader saw a red-underside Rossi, Tim—it is so, red is red, nude, raw as Red art.

Ungate me, Vic, I've met a gnu. / "Ungastroperitonitis—is it I? Not I," reports a gnu. [Two PDs.]

Well, Rae paid for one defoliated gift—ah, what fig-detail!—of Eden (or of Di) a pearl, Lew.

Well, Rae passed R.A. "Wet Stewardess" a pearl, Lew.

Went on Rowena: "Lo, I've not one viola, new or not new."

Won pots! Spa tympanists, I nap, my taps stop now!

Worse, *Kama Sutra*—sad loss, sold as art—USA makes row.

Yell up Elba car, O fallen Nella, for a cable-pulley.

Yes, a call, a bat, a ball, a Casey! / Yes act! A ball, a bat, Casey! / "Won't I help? Miss it in mad stab?" Yes, a Casey bats . . . Damn! It is simple—hit now! / Wonder Casey! Esteem meets eye—sacred now! / Yes, a clot! Sip, Isa, murder-red rum as I pistol Casey. [Five PDs.]

You bet I sure can omit Tim on a cerusite buoy!

Short Palindromic Sentences (letter-unit)

A design in Ruby burning is, Eda.

Aglow as Isis I saw Olga.

Aid and abet Amis as I mate bad Nadia.

A lob—a rap as bat stabs—a parabola!

A poem, a carol—or a cameo, Pa!

Are ponies, Iona, a *noise* in opera?

A tin mug for a jar of gum, Nita.

Basil is a b—!

Beware venom! Music I summon, ever a web!

Cora sees a roc. / Deer breed.

Dennis and Edna sinned.

Diana saw Dr. Awkward was an aid.

Di heard art—Strad. (Rae hid!)

Eda, my glass Algy made.

Edith, cold-eyed, eyed loch tide.

Eli, *votre* C no C, concerto vile!

Em, it's a periwig I wire—pastime!

Evil! A diamond, a cad—no maid alive!

Evil odes or prose do live.

Flesh! Saw I Mimi wash self!

Flesh? Sin if I finish self.

Girl (a mini-maid) Eva gave Di a minimal rig.

God, a slap! Paris, sir, appals a dog.

Go, fatal cello-doll! *Éclat?* A fog!

Here no orchestral arts, eh, crooner, eh?

He (*aside*); Sum amused Isa, eh?

Jar a tonga, nag not a Raj.

Kay, a red nude, peeped under a yak.

Kay dated a cadet, a Dyak.

La, not *atonal*!

Lager, sir, is regal.

Last fig—as a gift, Sal?

'll debase many names, a bed'll!

Loofahs awry at Ayr wash a fool.

Loot: slate, metal-plate, metal stool.

Madam's Adam's mad as Madam.

Ma handed Edna ham.

Man, Eve let an irate tar in at eleven a.m.

"Matting is level." Sign it, Tam.

Meek, I listen . . . No sonnets I like, Em.

Megan, I finish sin if I nag 'em.

Nigh table to hotel bath—gin!

No D? No L? .on.on? No, no! *LONDON!*

No, gird no maid a diamond rig on.

Not seven on a mere man, *one* vest on!

Nowise I bury rubies I won.

O desirable Melba, rise, do!

O had I nine more hero-men in Idaho!

O tarts! A castrato!

Otto made Ned a motto.

"Pupils!" I say as I slip up.

Pupils roll a ball or slip up.

Pure suet is opposite user-up.

Put Felix (I left) up.

Red rum, sir, is murder.
Reg, I tamed Em a tiger.
Re hypocrisy: as I say, sir, copy *her*.
Rise, take lame female Kate, sir.
Rot-corpse Sumatran art amuses proctor.
Sat in a taxi, left Felix at Anita's.
Snag royal! Piano, Mona? I play *organs*!
Stewed, a jade wets.
Swept pews. Yes, Sam Massey swept pews.
Tie soldier-trash (Sartre)—I'd lose it.
Ties ruck curse it!
To pistol? I pondered. No pilots I pot.
We name opera, rare poem, anew.
Won't Paganini nag apt now! / Yale ran a relay.
Yard notified, a jade I fit on dray.
Zen I bar, give lot to Levi, grab Inez.

Only a fraction of the English vocabulary is available to the
letter-unit palindrome. "Red" is utilized easily, but "blue" is not,
to give but one example. Lindon neatly circumvents this difficulty
by taking the word itself as the unit. There is, however, another set
of equally intractable difficulties attendant upon the construction
of word-unit palindromes.

PALINDROMIC SENTENCES (WORD-UNIT)

1. King, are you glad you are king?
2. What! So he is hanged, is he? So what?
3. So patient a doctor to doctor a patient so.
4. Company of fond people irks people fond of company.
5. Bomb-disposal squad with failed technique failed with squad-disposal bomb.
6. Girls, with boys passing, meet passing boys with girls.
7. Girl, bathing on Bikini, eyeing boy, finds boy eyeing bikini on bathing-girl.
8. You can cage a swallow, can't you, but you can't swallow a cage, can you!
9. Would I doubt you if away? Go away if you doubt I would.
10. Dollars make men covetous, then covetous men make dollars.
11. Fast ladies watching love scenes (such men!), hungry for love, *eat* love; for hungry men (such scenes!) love watching ladies fast.

12. Husband by murdered wife lies cold, and cold lies wife, murdered by husband.

13. Men wanted warning before police approached; squealer approached police before warning wanted men.

14. Women painted pretty pictures, such were they once; and once they were such pictures, pretty painted women!

15. Loved you that man? The kissing Nan saw I remembered; and remembered I saw Nan kissing the man that you loved.

16. Gliding is unearthly, ethereal, something you near when jumping, you see. (We certainly see. Certainly we see you jumping when near you something ethereal, unearthly is gliding!)

17. AMERICA TO SHIP A MAN TO MARS—from *Things of Tomorrow*. (Intention, perhaps; but perhaps intention tomorrow of Things from Mars to man a ship to America!)

18. Becoming very sure am I, looking—is Nora well?—around me, seeing beauty, that Nora is here. Is Nora that beauty seeing me around? Well, Nora is looking, I am sure, very becoming.

19. "To love?" she'd say. "Dare I and he—" Poor he! And I dare say she'd love to!

20. On radios with noisy speakers everywhere glass and china rattles; waiters, many of one race, move forks and knives, while knives and forks move, race; one of many waiters rattles china and glass, everywhere speakers noisy, with radios on . . .

The two following poems are palindromes in which the word is taken as the unit. For a third one, see the introduction.

LADIES LONG IN THE TOOTH

Widows ate wives once?
That believe I well.
Shadows on wives *pounce*,
Squat, where nearby crawl
    Others,
Eating, belching, eating . . .
    Others
Crawl nearby where, squat,
Pounce wives on shadows . . .
(Well, *I* believe that
Once wives ate widows!)

SPA

Laughing boys, legs bare, with girls bathing—
  Girls kind of fond are these,
Chaffing and cheering boys, limbs writhing . . .
   Swirls water, whips spume, splash seas,
    Breaking, into shrieking
     Girls . . .
      Noise and boys,
      Boys and noise . . .
      Girls,
     Shrieking, into breaking
    Seas splash, spume whips, water swirls . . .
Writhing limbs, boys cheering and chaffing—
  These are fond of kind girls,
Bathing girls with bare legs, boys laughing . . .

A letter written circa 1966 by J. A. Lindon contains the following passage:

REFLECTIONS ON EVE

. . . Eve's reply to Adam's self-introductory greeting was, I believe,
  "Eve. Foeman? Name of Eve."
Or, more explicitly,
  "Eve mine. Denied, under a ban, a bared nude in Eden, I'm
  Eve."
Or, perhaps:—
  "Eve—maiden name. Both sad in Eden? I dash to be manned,
  I am Eve!"
And, a little later:—
  "Eve mine. My hero! More Hymen! I'm Eve!"
  (Evidently she didn't even wait to introduce herself!)
Lilith of course had no such rapturous luck. She said hopefully:—
  "I'm alright, I Lilith. Girl am I."

She later went into more detail, but her concluding phrase showed
that it was all in vain. She said:—
  "Maid examined, I am a Miss 'All Right.' I, Lilith, girl, lass—
  I'm a maiden. (I'm axed, I am!)"

She did her best with old Adam, but he was a pigheaded chap, did just what he pleased, no sense at all. Thus

"He's got on—mad! A draught! I, Lilith, guard Adam—no togs, eh?"(And all she did was catch cold herself!)

"Did I sit in a draught? I, Lilith, guard an 'itis.' I did!"

Such reflections were to culminate ultimately in the following playlet, in which the dramatis personae speak entirely in (letter-unit) palindromes.

In Eden, I

ADAM: Madam—

EVE: Oh, who—

ADAM: (No girl-rig on!)

EVE: Heh?

ADAM: Madam, I'm Adam.

EVE: Name of a foeman?

ADAM: O stone me! Not so.

EVE: Mad! A maid I am, Adam.

ADAM: Pure, eh? Called Ella? Cheer up.

EVE: Eve, not Ella. Brat-star ballet on? Eve.

ADAM: Eve?

EVE: Eve, maiden name. Both sad in Eden? I dash to be manned, I am Eve.

ADAM: Eve. Drowsy baby's word. Eve.

EVE: Mad! A gift. I fit fig, Adam . . .

ADAM: On, hostess? Ugh! Gussets? Oh, no!

EVE: ? ? ?

ADAM: Sleepy baby *peels*.

EVE: Wolf! Low!

ADAM: Wolf? Fun, so snuff "low."

EVE: Yes, low! Yes, nil on, no linsey-wolsey!

ADAM: Madam, I'm *Adam*.

> *Named under a ban.*
> *A bared, nude man—*
>
> Aha!

EVE: Mad Adam!

ADAM: Mmmmmmmm!

EVE: Mmmmmmmm!

ADAM: Even in Eden I win Eden in Eve.

EVE: Pure woman in Eden, I win Eden in—a mower-up!

ADAM: Mmmmmmmm!

EVE: Adam, I'm Ada!

ADAM: Miss, I'm Cain, a monomaniac. Miss, I'm—

EVE: No, son.

ADAM: Name's Abel, a male base man.

EVE: Name not so, O stone man!

ADAM: Mad as it is it is Adam.

EVE: I'm a Madam Adam, am I?

ADAM: Eve?

EVE: Eve mine. Denied, a jade in Eden, I'm Eve.

ADAM: No fig. (Nor wrong if on!)

EVE: ???

ADAM: A daffodil I doff, Ada.

EVE: 'Tis a—what—ah, was it—

ADAM: Sun ever! A bare Venus . . .

EVE: 'S pity! So red, ungirt, rig-nude, rosy tips . . .

ADAM: Eve is a sieve!

EVE: Tut-tut!

ADAM: Now a see-saw on . . .

EVE: On me? (O poem!) No!

ADAM: Aha!

EVE: I won't! O not now, I—

ADAM: Aha!

EVE: NO! O God, I— (Fit if I do?) *Go on.*

ADAM: Hrrrrrrh!

EVE: Wow! Ow!

ADAM: Sores? (Alas, Eros!)

EVE: No, none. My hero! More hymen, on, on . . .

ADAM: Hrrrrrrrrrrrrrrrrrrrrrrh!

EVE: Revolting is error. Resign it, lover.

ADAM: No, not now I won't. On, on . . .

EVE: Rise, sir.

ADAM: Dewy dale, cinema-game . . . Nice lady wed?

EVE: Marry an Ayr ram!

ADAM: Rail on, O liar!

EVE: Live devil!

ADAM: Diamond-eyed no-maid!

BOTH: Mmmmmmmmmmmmmmmmmmmmmm!

Each of the following poems is a single, end-to-end palindrome, except those which are asterisked. In the latter poems each line is a separate palindrome.

IDA REPLIES

A dim or fond (as Asgard's set, so hailed)

"O tog not up, linen off,
It's a party, leg as I do!
Ida, had I fish to my name,
Soon nudies, legalists (?), *Eves*—"

(Ida rapt: "Oh!")

—"O Nimrod, animals!

If one mowed-under girl, lewder, is
Edified under it, tan-attired,
(Nude if I desired)
We'll rig red nude women of Islam
In a dorm in—O hot Paradise vests!"

(I lag, else I'd unnoose many moths!)

"If Ida had I—O Di, sagely trap a stiff one,
Nil put on, go to Delia! Hostess—"

Drags a sad "No" from Ida.

STACY'S SUPER-AWARE PUSSY-CATS

Pal?
Pal-pal?
(*Purrrrh!*)
Pals?

It's MIAOW
Tony
Cats
Sit, walk
Cats
Spill, lap milk

Eels
(Meek, ample)
Help make 'em
Sleek
Limp
All lips

Stack-law 'tis
Stacy
No two aims
'Tis
Lap . . .
(*Hrrrrup!*)
Lap, lap . . .
Lap . . .

STITCHES IN TIME

We sew.
Nell, Edna,
Ada—
(I
hem, eh?)
—Enid and Nadine
loop, spin, snip
"Damosel" silk, cut
elastic—"I'll iron,"
went on Sal.
"A ruffle's a slip!" I railed.
No, not to cod,
Di held e'en
Sharon's
pull-ups!
Norah's
needle hid?
Do cotton on, Delia!
Rip Ilsa's elf-fur—
alas, not new
nor illicit sale—
tuck lisle so mad,
pin, snip spool . . .

Enid and Nadine
hem, eh?
I,
Ada,
and Ellen,
we sew.

INTO THE UNKNOWN

Rise, cap!
Sniff oxygen . . .
Do orbits alter?
Cesta, rise!
No g—
Gyrator still upon
Sun, every gyre
Venus
No pull
It's rotary—
G gone, sir
At secret last I brood
Neg. yx . . .
Off in space, sir!

NOAH IN TROUBLE-SPOT

Slam in a den
Mad dogs I do
O gnus!
O rats!
O deer!

Feral lions
(No ill)
Are freed

O Star!
O Sun!

Good is God!

(Damned animals!)

WITHOUT RITES IN THE GARDEN*

Eve—No gift? Ah, what fig on Eve!—
Madam, name me man, Madam!
Evie, *ceremony*? No, me receive!
Mad as it is it is Adam!

NAUGHTY NATURISM!*

Ed, Una sees a nude—
No togs Eve's got on,
No Dot's pull-ups to don—
Dwell, ever revel lewd!

DRAW, O HOWARD

Draw, O hot moody sword girder-on!
Draw, or foot it! O negate wit! On!
Not I—wet age—not I! Too froward!
No red-rig drowsy doom to Howard!

AID FOR A SCANDINAVIAN ALCOHOLIC

Live, drab niggard!
Drug is for evil
Liver of Sigurd—
Drag gin, bar Devil!

HA! ON, ON, O NOAH!*

Eel-fodder, stack-cats red do flee
Ungotten, put up net to gnu,
I tip away a wapiti,
Ewer of miry rim for ewe.

VERSE DURING PRE-OP DELIRIUM

Ere Hera's empire's run—
(No, wears a hat severe!)
Ere Vesta has Rae won—
NURSE! "Rip-me's" are here!

ENEMY'S END*

Lived a foeman, name of a devil!
God, a foeman, name of a dog!
Level, erased, ah, shades are level!
Go from life, sir—rise film or fog!

PICNIC

Tangle peril, Lew—
   Wet stones I rebel at—
Tale be: Rise not, stew!
   Well I repel gnat.

ABDUCTION*

Bargees I see grab
Nell, Edna and Ellen!
Bandits, avast! I'd nab
No "lefties"—oppose it, felon!

AWAY WITH THAT TABLE-GAME!*

Deb abed,
Pusses sup . . .
Den, Lil, Ned,
Put it up!

AT THE SEASIDE*

Eva can, I see, bone no bees in a cave,
  "Delia was ill!" Lisa wailed;
Eva wondered "No pier?" ere I pondered "No wave?"
  Delia sits, a petite. Past I sailed.

BLACK AND WHITE*

Lived as a dog—O no! God, as a devil!
Doom lives ever, it's astir, Eve's evil mood.
Live, O Devil, revel ever, live, do evil!
(Do, O God, no evil deed, live on, do good!)

Nonsense!*

Debate what? Now in Eden I won't—ah!—wet a bed!
Definitely, Leno, not on *one* "Lyle" tin I fed!
Deirdre, ta! We most eye no one, yet some water dried!
Ed, I woo! Tim, Allan, Eden all—am I too wide?

Finally, presented here for your delectation, are two superb palindromic poems in which the line is taken as the unit:

As I Was Passing . . .

As I was passing near the jail
I met a man, but hurried by.
His face was ghastly, grimly pale.
He had a gun. I wondered why
He had. A gun? I wondered . . . why,
His face was *ghastly*! Grimly pale,
I met a man, but hurried by,
As I was passing near the jail.

Doppelgänger

I   Entering the lonely house with my wife
      I saw him for the first time
    Peering furtively from behind a bush—
        Blackness that moved,
      A shape amid the shadows,
    A momentary glimpse of gleaming eyes
      Revealed in the ragged moon.
    A closer look (he seemed to turn) might have
    Put him to flight forever—
      I dared not
    (For reasons that I failed to understand),
      Though I knew I should act at once.

II   I puzzled over it, hiding alone,
    Watching the woman as she neared the gate.
      He came, and I saw him crouching
        Night after night.
        Night after night
      He came, and I saw him crouching,
    Watching the woman as she neared the gate.

III   I puzzled over it, hiding alone—
        Though I knew I should act at once,
    For reasons that I failed to understand
        I dared not
        Put him to flight forever.

IV   A closer look (he seemed to turn) might have
        Revealed in the ragged moon
    A momentary glimpse of gleaming eyes,
        A shape amid the shadows,
        Blackness that moved.

V   Peering furtively from behind a bush,
        I saw him, for the first time,
    Entering the lonely house with my wife.

SOURCES OF ANAGRAMS

The names and pseudonyms of some authors of the anagrams have been abbreviated as follows:

A = Amaranth.
DCV = D. C. Ver.
EB = Erik Bodin of Norfolk, Va.
GBK = Geo. B. King.
HWB = Howard W. Bergerson.
M = Molemi.
PJF = Patrick J. Flavin of Dorchester, Mass.
R = Remardo.
V = Viking.

The journal abbreviations are:

AP = Ardmore Puzzler.
C = Complications.
EE = Eastern Enigma.
E = Enigma.
NP = Newark Puzzler.

Date unknown is abbreviated "d.u." and no data is "un."

1. PJF, 1935. **2.** Margaretta, *C*, July 25, 1906. **3.** PJF, 1935. **4.** Randolph, d.u. **5.** un. **6.** HWB, *Word Ways*, Feb., 1969. **7.** EB, 1932. **8.** V. **9.** V. **10.** M, *E*, June, 1920. **11.** Jemand, *E*, Nov., 1923. **12.** Bolis, d.u. **13.** GBK, 1934. **14.** un. **15.** GBK, 1935. **16.** un. **17.** (a) V. (b) GBK, 1932. **18.** Hercules B. McPherrin, Denver, 1933. **19.** Arty Ess, *C*, April 4, 1906. **20.** Ellsworth, *E*, Feb., 1924. **21.** P. Chinn, *E*, Oct., 1916. **22.** un. **23.** E. S. Crow, *E*, Jan., 1914. **24.** A, *E*, Nov., 1912. **25.** A, *E*, Dec., 1912. **26.** GBK, 1932. **27.** DCV, *EE*, Dec., 1903. **28.** DCV, d.u. **29.** GBK, 1932. **30.** V. **31.** Gen. E. Norre, *Thedom*, Nov. 15, 1895. **32.** Morris Better, Detroit, 1932. **33.** EB, 1932. **34.** Park, *NP*, July 9, 1905. **35.** GBK, 1932. **36.** Hercules, *E*, July, 1924. **37.** EB, 1932. **38.** un. **39.** Nox, *The Brighton Item*, Aug. 21, 1915. **40.** GBK, 1934. **41.** Dmitri A. Borgmann, *Language on Vacation*, Scribner's, 1965. **42.** un. **43.** Lateo, *E*, March, 1914. **44.** PJF, 1932. **45.** A, *C*, Jan. 13, 1911. **46.** A, *Enigmatic Oddities*, Oct. 6, 1901. **47.** Kenneth,

C, Jan. 31, 1899. **48.** Lord Baltimore, *Mystery*, Feb. 6, 1896. **49.** Ellsworth, *B&O Magazine*, March, 1925. **50.** un.
51. (a) A, *E*, Aug., 1913. (b) A, *E*, Nov., 1925. **52.** un. **53.** Loris B. Curtis, Mason, Mich., 1932. **54.** King Carnival, *Telegraph Twisters*, 1905. **55.** un. **56.** F. J. Kathman, Cincinnati, 1932. **57.** Ess Ell, *NP*, June 2, 1906. **58.** PJF, 1936. **59.** EB, 1933. **60.** GBK, 1935. **61.** E. J. Rodden, Philadelphia, 1934. **62.** M, *Oracle*, Jan., 1907. **63.** A, *E*, Aug., 1926. **64.** S. James Nesi, New York, 1936. **65.** Busbecq, *Golden Days Puzzledom*, Sept. 14, 1891. **66.** Balmar, *Perplexities*, April 7, 1900. **67.** Hercules B. McPherrin, Denver, 1932. **68.** Mrs. Hector Rosenfeld, New York, 1933. **69.** (a) Author unknown, *Farmers' Almanac*, 1821. (b) un. **70.** Mabel P., *Enigmatic Oddities*, April 17, 1900. **71.** HWB, *Word Ways*, Nov., 1969. **72.** un. **73.** Wanderoo, *E*, Jan., 1920. **74.** A, *Enigmatic Oddities*, d.u. **75.** A, *E*, Oct., 1910.
76. Sam Weller, *AP*, July 1, 1903. **77.** DCV, *The Mystic Tree*, Feb., 1899. **78.** Spica, *E*, Nov., 1913. **79.** Arcanus, *NP*, April 28, 1907. **80.** M. **81.** Mrs. E. B. M. Wortman, Jackson Heights, N.Y., 1932. **82.** Jemand, *E*, Jan., 1924. **83.** Tom A. Hawk, *C*, Feb. 25, 1902. **84.** Ned Hazel, *New Jersey Puzzler*, Nov., 1883. **85.** Le Dare, *E*, Oct., 1918. **86.** Sylvia, *NP*, July 30, 1905. **87.** Darryl H. Francis, Hounslow, Middlesex, England, *Word Ways*, Nov., 1968. **88.** J. E. Reizenstein, Iowa City, Iowa, 1935. **89.** Enavlicm, *E*, July, 1920. **90.** Jason, *E*, Nov., 1912. **91.** Jemand, *E*, Sept., 1915. **92.** Alcyo, *E*, Feb., 1925. **93.** Arcanus, *Oracle*, Dec., 1906. **94.** William G. Bryan, Greenfield, Mass., 1935. **95.** Arcanus, *E*, Nov., 1912. **96.** HWB. **97.** Quebig, *NP*, July 28, 1906. **98.** A, *E*, Nov., 1910. **99.** Kee Pon, *E*, Dec., 1917. **100.** R, *Oracle*, May, 1909. **101.** Arty Ess, *C*, May 10, 1905. **102.** PJF, 1936. **103.** GBK, 1934. **104.** Alcyo, *Thedom*, May 1, 1881. **105.** Kosciusko McGinty, *EE*, Dec., 1898. **106.** (a) Atlantis, *Brighton Item*, Nov. 2, 1914. (b) Moonshine, *E*, Jan., 1918. **107.** Sam Weller, *The Eurekan*, Feb., 1903. **108.** William Lutwiniak, Jersey City, N.J., 1935. **109.** A, *E*, Feb., 1911. **110.** (a) PJF, 1935. (b) Gemini, *E*, Dec., 1924. **111.** Erien, *Mystic Argosy*, Jan. 13, 1900. **112.** L.Z.H., *E*, Aug., 1921. **113.** EB, 1932. **114.** PJF, 1935. **115.** Loris B. Curtis, Mason, Mich., 1932. **116.** Swamp Angel, *C*, July 31, 1908. **117.** (a) R, *C*, April 30, 1909. (b) Balmar, *E*, June, 1910. **118.** Phil, *Enigmatic Oddities*, Nov. 30, 1902. **119.** David Shulman, New York, 1935. **120.** Jack o' Lantern, *E*, July, 1926. **121.** Argyle, *Golden Days*, Oct. 15, 1881. **122.** J. E. Reizenstein, Iowa City, Iowa, 1935. **123.** Roscoe, *E*, May, 1919. **124.** un. **125.** un.
126. Atlantis, d.u. **127.** J. W. Davis, Albany, N.Y., 1932. **128.** Damaskus, *Mystic Argosy*, Feb. 19, 1898. **129.** E. J. Rodden, Philadelphia, 1932. **130.** Resolute, *Oracle*, Oct., 1903. **131.** Resolute, *NP*, March 10, 1906. **132.** A, *E*, July, 1924. **133.** A, *E*, April, 1918. **134.** (a) Jemand, *E*, April, 1924. (b) N. Jineer, *E*, April, 1924. **135.** un. **136.** DCV, *C*, Aug. 21, 1900. **137.** un. **138.** Nelsonian, *C*, May 23, 1906. **139.** Alan Wayne, New York, 1935. **140.** Camillius, *Golden Days*, May 5, 1883. **141.** Hector Rosenfeld, New York, 1932. **142.** Hercules. **143.** A, *E*, Dec., 1910. **144.** Dick Ens, *The Mystic Art*, Sept. 18, 1885. **145.** (a) un. (b) A.L.S., *AP*, Aug. 1, 1905. **146.** A, *B&O Magazine*, Dec., 1924. **147.** Kee Pon, *E*, March, 1914. **148.** A, *E*, Nov., 1912. **149.** un. **150.** (a) A, *E*, Dec., 1910. (b) un.
151. Jason, *Oracle*, Jan., 1906. **152.** Stocles, *AP*, July 1, 1904. **153.** Remardo, *E*, May, 1915. **154.** W. A. Moore, Denville, N.J., 1933. **155.** William G. Bryan, Greenfield, Mass., 1935. **156.** Eureka, *E*, Oct., 1924. **157.** Pax, *E*, Aug., 1917. **158.** M, *C*, Jan. 19, 1912. **159.** un. **160.** Skeeziks, *The Study*, Nov. 1, 1893. **161.** M.C.S., *C*, Dec. 26, 1899. **162.** J. S. Tennant, New York, 1932. **163.** Hercules, *E*, Oct., 1924. **164.** Enavlicm, *NP*, Jan. 5, 1907.

165. un. **166.** Nox, *The Brighton Item*, Oct. 18, 1913. **167.** Atlantis, *E*, March, 1925. **168.** R, *Oracle*, Feb., 1908. **169.** A, *E*, Feb., 1916. **170.** Alec Sander, *E*, Feb., 1925. **171.** A, *Enigmatic Oddities*, Jan. 29, 1904. **172.** A, *E*, Oct., 1913. **173.** un. **174.** A, *E*, July, 1913. **175.** DCV, *E*, June, 1919. **176.** Mrs. Harris, *Mystic Laurels*, Sept. 3, 1885. **177.** Anise Lang, *The Mazy Masker*, Oct., 1887. **178.** un. **179.** R, *E*, June, 1919. **180.** R, *E*, Oct., 1917. **181.** E. J. Rodden, Philadelphia, 1933. **182.** Tryon, *E*, April, 1913. **183.** Sam Weller, *EE*, 1898. **184.** Nelsonian, *Mysteriarchy*, March 10, 1887. **185.** GBK, 1936. **186.** Emma Line, *E*, March, 1916. **187.** Hyperion, *C*, June 8, 1904. **188.** Phil Down, *The Lakeshore Poser*, July, 1887. **189.** Jack o' Lantern, *Golden Days*, July 18, 1891. **190.** un. **191.** Phil O. Sopher, *Eusama*, Jan., 1894. **192.** Mrs. John Matthews, Lenox, Mass., 1935. **193.** (a) Hercules B. McPherrin, Denver, 1935. (b) Spica, *E*, Oct., 1914. (c) Atlantis, *E*, Oct., 1914. **194.** Jemand, *E*, Feb., 1914. **195.** M, *NP*, Feb., 1908. **196.** Ajax, *E*, May, 1926. **197.** un. **198.** Author unknown, Walsh's *Handbook of Literary Curiosities*, 1892. **199.** Jason, *Oracle*, June, 1905. **200.** Rayle Rhoder, *E*, July, 1926.

201. Nypho, *E*, March, 1913. **202.** A, *E*, Dec., 1913. **203.** Tippecanoe, *AP*, Aug. 31, 1899. **204.** (a) L.Z.H., *E*, May, 1922. (b) Primrose, *E*, July, 1922. **205.** George Lamb, Burton, Ohio, 1935. **206.** R, June, 1923. **207.** A, *E*, Feb., 1911. **208.** M.C.S., *B&O Magazine*, Aug., 1925. **209.** Jim Jam, *EE*, Dec., 1898. **210.** Bolis, *Golden Days*, Nov. 8, 1884. **211.** Dreamer, *E*, Feb., 1926. **212.** Delian, *C*, June 19, 1907. **213.** Scretaw, *Golden Days*, April 24, 1897. **214.** Arcanus, *C*, April 3, 1908. **215.** Gi Gantic, *Golden Days*, Feb. 1, 1900. **216.** W. E. Stern, *Perplexities*, April 28, 1900. **217.** Emma Line, *E*, June, 1910. **218.** Ivanhoe, "The Enigma" (*American Farmer*), June 25, 1894. **219.** C. Saw, *AP*, July 27, 1899. **220.** David Shulman, New York, 1935. **221.** Q., *C*, April 5, 1912. **222.** un. **223.** Helva Goodman, *E*, March, 1916. **224.** (a) Laudy Daw, *Mystery*, Aug. 25, 1892. (b) A, *In Mystic Mood*, July, 1911. (c) PJF, 1935. **225.** Viking.

226. Dr. Arthur Kleykamp, St. Louis, 1935. **227.** un. **228.** un. **229.** Remlap, *EE*, Dec., 1898. **230.** Anonyme, *E*, Oct., 1921. **231.** I. M. Wise, *AP*, March 16, 1901. **232.** Dorothy Doolittle, *Detroit Puzzler*, April, 1894. **233.** Sitt Downe, d.u. **234.** A, *E*, Nov., 1910. **235.** Sir A., *E*, June, 1917. **236.** A, *E*, June, 1926. **237.** un. **238.** Hermit, *Golden Days*, July 4, 1885. **239.** Alexander, *E*, July, 1923. **240.** Air Raid, *E*, April, 1920. **241.** Alexander, *Telegraphic Twisters*, 1905. **242.** Byrnhec, *EE*, Dec., 1898. **243.** Binks, *EE*, Dec., 1903. **244.** A, *E*, April, 1925. **245.** Ellsworth, d.u. **246.** Arcanus, *Oracle*, Oct., 1907. **247.** Violet, *NP*, March 9, 1907. **248.** Dr. Arthur Kleykamp, St. Louis, 1935. **249.** GBK, 1935. **250.** A, *E*, Dec., 1910.

251. A, d.u. **252.** A, *E*, Nov., 1910. **253.** O.N.E. One, *Golden Days*, Nov. 2, 1902. **254.** Spreggs, *E*, May, 1915. **255.** Balmar, *C*, Nov. 20, 1900. **256.** Roscoe, *E*, Jan., 1918. Viking. **257.** un. **258.** E. S. Crow, *E*, Feb., 1911. **259.** A, *E*, Feb., 1926. **260.** A, *E*, April, 1925. **261.** Author unknown, *Notes and Queries*, London, England, 1851 et seq. **262.** Chris, *E*, March, 1915. **263.** Fred Domino, *C*, Oct. 29, 1909. **264.** Arty Ess, *AP*, Aug. 15, 1907. **265.** J.E.W., *Mystery*, March 21, 1895. **266.** Sphinx, *AP*, Feb., 1907. **267.** A, *E*, Feb., 1917. **268.** M, *In Mystic Mood*, Nov., 1909. **269.** Bolis, *EE*, Dec., 1898. **270.** un. **271.** Spica, *E*, May, 1913. **272.** T.H., *C*, May 2, 1899. **273.** (a) Aspiricus, *EE*, Dec., 1898. (b) Robert Hooke, Pittsburgh, Pa., 1935. **274.** Viking. **275.** Author unknown, *John o' London*, London, d.u.

276. Hercules, *E*, d.u. **277.** Enavlicm, *E*, Dec., 1917. **278.** M.C.S., *C*, Oct. 15, 1901. **279.** Francolin, *Brighton Item*, Sept. 4, 1915. **280.** A, *E*, Sept., 1924. **281.** Polly Gram, *Nonplustics*, 1896. **282.** Dauntless, *NP*, 1908. **283.**

Atlas, *Mystic Argosy*, Feb. 19, 1898. **284.** un. **285.** Enavlicm, *NP*, Jan. 12, 1907. **286.** Arcanus, *E*, Dec., 1914. **287.** A, *C*, April 7, 1911. **288.** Amor, *B&O Magazine*, June, 1925. **289.** Art, *Queer Quizzes*, Aug. 11, 1912. **290.** A, *E*, June, 1924. **291.** Atlantis, *E*, March, 1912. **292.** H.W.B. **293.** A, *C*, Jan. 3, 1913. **294.** un. **295.** Aspiro, *C*, Feb. 24, 1903. **296.** Jemand, *E*, Dec., 1924. **297.** Kenneth, *C*, March 7, 1899. **298.** A, *B&O Magazine*, April, 1926. **299.** Moonshine, *EE List*, Dec., 1898. **300.** Enavlicm, *E*, Feb., 1922. **301.** Martin Gardner. **302.** R, *E*, April, 1915. **303.** A, *E*, June, 1924. **304.** *E*, June, 1917. **305.** un. **306.** Jo Mullins, *AP*, Sept. 23, 1899. **307.** un. **308.** Nypho, d.u. **309.** Nyas, *Mystery*, March 14, 1895. **310.** Jason, *The Sphinx*, June, 1901. **311.** Balmar, *C*, Dec. 18, 1900. **312.** J.C.M., *EE List*, Dec., 1898. **313.** Jo Mullins, *Brighton Item*, Dec. 12, 1914. **314.** Arty Fishel, *NP*, Feb. 24, 1906. **315.** Abel Em, *Oracle*, Sept. 1905. **316.** HWB. **317.** Arty Ess, *E*, Oct., 1920. **318.** L.M.N. Terry, *EE List*, Dec., 1898. **319.** Tom A. Hawk, *C*, Nov. 4, 1903. **320.** Lord Baltimore, *Perplexities*, Feb. 11, 1898. **321.** GBK, 1934. **322.** EB, 1934. **323.** Cincinnatus, *Merion Maze*, 1898. **324.** Ace, *E*, Nov., 1912. **325.** A, *E*, March, 1915. **326.** Anonyme, *Oracle*, Jan. 15, 1896. **327.** PJF, 1935. **328.** Sub Rosa, *The Study*, Jan. 7, 1888. **329.** M, *AP*, Oct. 1, 1908. **330.** Kenneth, *C*, Feb. 7, 1899. **331.** George C. Lamb, Burton, Ohio, 1934. **332.** Enavlicm, *E*, Nov., 1917. **333.** M, *E*, Nov., 1910. **334.** n.d. **335.** A, *E*, Dec., 1924. **336.** F. Rederick, *AP*, Aug. 31, 1899. **337.** Roscoe, *E*, July, 1923. **338.** Lord Baltimore, *Mystery*, Feb. 20, 1896. **339.** EB, 1935. **340.** Ellsworth, *E*, May, 1925. **341.** un. **342.** DCV, *EE*, Dec., 1898. **343.** un. **344.** un. **345.** Delaware, *Telegraph Twisters*, July, 1905. **346.** Hyperion, *C*, Dec. 6, 1905. **347.** un. **348.** Walsh's *Handbook of Literary Curiosities*. **349.** Lord Baltimore, *Perplexities*, Aug. 14, 1896. **350.** (a) Hercules, *E*, July, 1926. (b) PJF, 1935. **351.** M, *In Mystic Mood*, Nov., 1911. **352.** (a) William G. Bryan, Greenfield, Mass., 1935. (b) O.N.E. One, *NP*, August 13, 1905. **353.** M, *E*, Dec., 1920. **354.** Saxon, *C*, April 22, 1902. **355.** A, *Enigmatic Oddities*, March 23, 1902. **356.** HWB. **357.** Tunste, *E*, Jan., 1911. **358.** Eureka, *E*, Oct., 1924. **359.** Hi Kerr, *E*, June, 1926. **360.** L.Z.H., *E*, Sept., 1924. **361.** Walsh's *Handbook of Literary Curiosities*. **362.** A, *E*, Nov., 1924. **363.** Atlantis, *E*, Aug., 1912. **364.** Al, *E*, Sept., 1925. **365.** A, *E*, June, 1916. **366.** A, *E*, Feb., 1913. **367.** Published Jan., 1920, in a puzzle magazine of uncertain identity. (*Enigma?*) **368.** R, *E*, July, 1917. **369.** un. **370.** St. Germaine, *AP*, Aug. 17, 1899. **371.** Nypho, *E*, Aug., 1911. **372.** Atlantis, *E*, Dec., 1914. **373.** un. **374.** A, *AP*, July 1, 1907. **375.** M.C.S., *C*, Dec., 8, 1911. **376.** un. **377.** un. **378.** Mr. and Mrs. Hector Rosenfeld, New York, 1934. **379.** M, *AP*, June 1, 1906. **380.** Eureka, *Mystic Tree*, April 5, 1888. **381.** un. **382.** John H. Howard, Arcadia, Mich., 1932. **383.** Sam Weller, *EE*, Dec., 1898. **384.** Rex Ford, *E*, Sept., 1901. **385.** Sam Weller, *Salmagundi*, Feb., 1883. **386.** M, Sept. 1, 1906. **387.** Arty Fishel, *EE*, Dec., 1898. **388.** DCV, *E*, June, 1913. **389.** GBK, 1935. **390.** Frankolin, *E*, Jan., 1915. **391.** Justa Parson, *AP*, Oct. 15, 1905. **392.** un. **393.** M.C.S., *C*, April 29, 1910. **394.** HWB. **395.** Atlas, *E*, Nov., 1910. **396.** Criss Cross, *Golden Days*, Jan. 5, 1898. **397.** Carroll, *In Mystic Mood*, Jan., 1911. **398.** Violet, *NP*, Jan., 1908. **399.** PJF, 1935. **400.** M.C.S., *C*, Dec. 24, 1908. **401.** DCV, *Puzzlers' Review*, March, 1902. **402.** Neophyte, *NP*, Aug. 4, 1906. **403.** un. **404.** Walsh's *Handbook of Literary Curiosities*. **405.** V, *E*, 1934. **406.** P.A.B., *E*, Jan., 1922. **407.** Balmar, *Perplexities*, March 2, 1900. **408.** Alan Wayne, New York, 1935. **409.** Hyperion, *C*, May 15, 1900. **410.** HWB. **411.** Holden, *Notes and Queries*, Aug. 27, 1851. **412.** Q., *E*, Dec., 1920. **413.** A, *E*,

Nov., 1912. **414.** Mark Tapley, *EE*, Dec., 1898. **415.** A, *E*, July, 1924. **416.**
PJF, 1936. **417.** A, *E*, June, 1924. **418.** Lie Lay, *The Hermit and Crypt*, Sept.,
1898. **419.** Gemini, *E*, July, 1924. **420.** After All, *AP*, Aug. 15, 1902. **421.**
Arcanus, *C*, March 13, 1900. **422.** La Noitan, *E*, Dec., 1913. **423.** Ralph, *AP*,
Nov. 15, 1906. **424.** Evening Star, *Telegraph Twisters*, June, 1905. **425.** un.
426. M.C.S., *C*, Feb. 12, 1901. **427.** K.T. Did, *E*, May, 1923. **428.**
Skeeziks, *Thedom*, Feb. 1, 1889. **429.** Enavlicm, *E*, Jan., 1922. **430.** A, *E*, June,
1924. **431.** Jemand. **432.** Alec Sander, *E*, July, 1922. **433.** un. **434.** Arty
Ess, *C*, April 5, 1905. **435.** O.N.E. One, *NP*, Oct. 13, 1906. **436.** O.N.E. One,
NP, Oct. 13, 1905. **437.** Morris Better, Detroit, 1933. **438.** Phil Down, *The
Mystic Taps*, June 10, 1891. **439.** Frank G. Mills, Banning, Cal., 1932. **440.** un.
441. A, *E*, Nov., 1912. **442.** J. H. Wickham, Jr., Baltimore, 1936. **443.** Spud,
E, Dec., 1922. **444.** Balmar, *AP*, May 25, 1900. **445.** A, *C*, April 7, 1911.
446. A, *E*, Oct., 1924. **447.** Beech Nut, *Golden Days*, April 27, 1889. **448.**
Nelsonian, *C*, April 18, 1906. **449.** Lateo, *E*, March, 1924. **450.** (a) M.C.S.,
C, Feb. 28, 1899. (b) Balmar, *AP*, May 26, 1900. (c) Barnyard, *E*, Aug., 1921.
451. Balmar, *Perplexities*, Jan. 6, 1900. **452.** Esperance, *AP*, July 15, 1902.
453. Ralph, *C*, June 3, 1902. **454.** HWB. **455.** Hercules, *E*. **456.** (a) R, *In
Mystic Mood*, Nov., 1910. (b) A, *E*, Dec., 1916. **457.** Ellsworth, *E*, Jan., 1925.
458. A, *E*, Sept., 1924. **459.** Rex, *AP*, March 3, 1900. **460.** M.C.S.. *C*, Dec. 24,
1901. **461.** Cincinnatus, *Merion Maze*, Sept., 1898. **462.** Atlantis, *E*, July, 1924.
463. DCV, *Diamond Club Courier*, Aug., 1898. **464.** Author unknown, *Notes and
Queries*, London, 1851. **465.** Traddles, *Our Mystical Medley*, Nov., 1886. **466.**
Walsh's *Handbook of Literary Curiosities*. **467.** R, *E*, March, 1915. **468.** Welred,
The Black Imp, Feb., 1899. **469.** Arcanus, *Mystery*, Feb. 27, 1896. **470.** Em
Jay, *E*, Nov., 1923. **471.** Lord Baltimore, *Mystery*, Nov. 5, 1891. **472.** Gee, *E*,
Dec., 1912. **473.** GBK, 1934. **474.** Nypho, *E*, Dec., 1925. **475.** A.L.S., *AP*,
Jan., 1903.

476. HWB. **477.** Hercules, *E*. **478.** Hercules, *E*. **479.** Bolis (appeared
Key to Puzzledom, 1908, but first published earlier). **480.** A, *Enigmatic Oddities*,
Oct. 20, 1901. **481.** Jo Mullins, *AP*, July 17, 1899. **482.** Nobel Holderread,
Milford, Ind., 1933. **483.** Kenneth, *E*, March, 1926. **484.** O.N.E. One, *NP*,
Sept. 2, 1907. **485.** O. Possum, *The Round Table*, Nov., 1879. **486.** un. **487.**
John H. Howard, Arcadia, Mich., 1935. **488.** EB, 1932. **489.** un. **490.**
Hercules, *C*, 1894. **491.** Emma Line, *E*, May, 1914. **492.** F. I. Nance, *E*,
June, 1919. **493.** (a) Sam Weller, *Golden Days*, July 2, 1881. (b) PJF, 1935.
494. un. **495.** Sir Urian, *C*, July 5, 1898. **496.** Ralph, *The Sphinx*, May, 1901.
497. A, d.u. **498.** Francolin, *E*, Nov., 1915. **499.** Lord Baltimore, *The Study*,
Feb., 1892. **500.** un.

501. PJF, 1936. **502.** DCV, *E*, May, 1920. **503.** Hexagony, *C*, June 12,
1908. **504.** Ace, *E*, Aug., 1912. **505.** un. **506.** O.N.E. One, *NP*, Feb. 2, 1909.
507. Jemand, *E*, Dec., 1915. **508.** Elia, Jr., *Master Puzzler* contribution, not
previously published. **509.** M, d.u. **510.** M, *B&O Magazine*, Feb., 1924.
511. R. P. Woodman, New York, 1933. **512.** (a) Ace, *Mystic Argosy*, March 21,
1898. (b) Jason, *The Sphinx*, May, 1901. **513.** Delian, *The Sphinx*, May, 1901.
514. Hercules, *E*, June, 1924. **515.** Bolis, *EE*, Dec., 1898. **516.** Ef Fen, *EE*,
Dec., 1898. **517.** M, *E*, Feb., 1911. **518.** PJF, 1935. **519.** S. James Nesi, New
York, 1936. **520.** Francolin, *E*, Feb., 1917. **521.** Mrs. Mabel V. McKeown,
Chicago, 1935. **522.** St. Germaine, *The Mystic Tree*, March, 1898. **523.** Nypho,
E, Aug., 1913. **524.** Skeeziks, *Puzzle Calls*, Feb. 21, 1888. **525.** A. Cyril
Pearson, *The Twentieth Century Book of Puzzles*.

526. C.A.R., *C*, June 6, 1913. **527.** un. **528.** Nox, *The Brighton Item*, Aug.
9, 1913. **529.** Q., *E*, Oct., 1921. **530.** Q., *E*, Oct., 1910. **531.** un. **532.**

DCV, *The Oracle*, Nov., 1906. **533.** Leonard Shapiro, West Warwick, R.I., 1935. **534.** *Telegraph Twisters*, Jan. 6, 1906. **535.** DCV, *E*, April, 1913. **536.** (a) Walsh's *Handbook of Literary Curiosities*. (b) Gwendoline, *C*, Sept. 5, 1897. **537.** PJF, 1935. **538.** Enavlicm, *NP*, June, 1908. **539.** V. **540.** Kenneth, *E*, Dec., 1925. **541.** O. Range, *The Key*, Aug., 1891. **542.** Spica, *C*, Aug. 5, 1902. **543.** EB, 1933. **544.** (a) M. O. Wellman, Lansing, Mich., 1932. (b) DCV, *EE*, Dec., 1898. **545.** Atlantis, d.u. **546.** GBK, 1933. **547.** Binks, *Merion Maze*, Jan. 12, 1899. **548.** (a) un. (b) N. J. Neer, *B&O Magazine*, Dec., 1924. **549.** HWB. **550.** un.

551. Balmar, *The Mystic Argosy*, Oct. 4, 1902. **552.** Jason, *AP*, March 3, 1900. **553.** Skeeziks, *C*, Jan. 15, 1896. **554.** Resolute, *C*, May 30, 1906. **555.** EZ2C, *EE*, Dec., 1898. **556.** un. **557.** M.C.S., *AP*, March 15, 1903. **558.** Bolis, *EE*, Dec., 1898. **559.** Enavlicm, *E*, Jan., 1920. **560.** Ithaca, *Arcana*, Sept. 29, 1887. **561.** J. E. Reizenstein, Iowa City, Iowa, 1935. **562.** un. **563.** Kenneth, *B&O Magazine*, Oct., 1925. **564.** un. **565.** Bolis, *Golden Days*, Nov. 7, 1885. **566.** GBK, 1933. **567.** Arty Ess, *E*, May, 1910. **568.** (a) Nettie H., *EE*, Dec., 1898. (b) Anise Lang, *AP*, Dec. 15, 1902. **569.** Chester A. Griffin, Franklin, N.H., 1934. **570.** Sphinx, *AP*, Feb. 16, 1901. **571.** V, *E*. **572.** R, *E*, Nov., 1919. **573.** Al T. Tude, d.u. **574.** (a) A, *E*, Nov., 1911. (b) un. **575.** Atlantis, *E*, Feb., 1915.

576. DCV, *EE*, Dec., 1893. **577.** Nelsonian, *Enigmatic Oddities*, 1900. **578.** Hyperion, *C*, March 23, 1904. **579.** Jason, *AP*, May 15, 1905. **580.** A, *E*, Feb., 1913. **581.** Eruditus, *Thedom*, Feb. 10, 1890. **582.** (a) V. (b) *E*, Nov., 1912. (c) Donatello, *E*, Feb., 1913. **583.** Lord Baltimore, *Mystic Tree*, Sept., 1899. **584.** EB, 1934. **585.** un. **586.** Tranza, *C*, Oct. 23, 1908. **587.** un. **588.** Jack O'Lantern, *Golden Days*, June 1, 1899. **589.** William Lutwiniak, Jersey City, 1935. **590.** Hercules, *E*, June, 1926. **591.** un. **592.** Shoo Fly, *Quillets*, Aug., 1896. **593.** HWB. **594.** Al T. Tude, *E*, Aug., 1923. **595.** un. **596.** A, *E*, Jan., 1924. **597.** C.A.H., *C*, Nov. 17, 1911. **598.** Fred W. Leipziger, Detroit, 1933. **599.** Golightly, *Golden Days*, Oct. 29, 1887. **600.** A, *C*, Jan. 13, 1911.

601. un. **602.** un. **603.** Hercules. **604.** Anonyme, *Oracle*, Jan., 1907. **605.** Bolis, *EE*, Dec., 1898. **606.** Sphinx, *AP*, April 1, 1902. **607.** Earnest, *Oracle*, July, 1905. **608.** EB, 1934. **609.** Arcanus, *AP*, April 1, 1908. **610.** Hercules. **611.** Hercules. **612.** DCV, *AP*, Nov. 25, 1899. **613.** L. M. N. Terry, *AP*, Oct. 13, 1900. **614.** Alec Sander, *E*, July, 1919. **615.** Atlantis, *E*, July, 1924. **616.** Ralph, *C*, Jan. 28, 1902. **617.** A, *E*, May, 1925. **618.** un. **619.** DCV, *E*, Sept., 1915. **620.** (a) un. (b) Dr. J. E. C. Snyder, Hoboken, N.J., 1934. **621.** George C. Lamb, Burton, Ohio, 1932. **622.** Chris, *E*, Sept., 1917. **623.** un. **624.** Quebig, *NP*, Feb. 4, 1889. **625.** John O' London, d.u.

626. (a) Bolis, *Our Deep Perplexities*, Jan., 1887. (b) Asian, *The Mystic Knight*, Sept., 1879. **628.** *Farmers' Almanac*, 1812. **629.** Rusticus, *E*, April, 1912. **630.** Traddles, *EE*, Dec., 1898. **631.** Nypho, *E*, Jan., 1925. **632.** Phonog, *Mystery*, June 29, 1893. **633.** Abel Em, *The Eurekan*, Dec., 1904. **634.** M.C.S., *E*, Aug., 1910. **635.** Elsie, *E*, Nov. 11, 1915. **636.** Ahmed, *Our Mystic Circle*, June, 1887. **637.** (a) Nypho, *E*, Dec., 1925. (b) Hercules, *E*, March, 1925. **638.** (a) GBK, 1934. (b) un. **639.** un. **640.** un. **641.** T.H., *AP*, Dec. 15, 1908. **642.** A, *B&O Magazine*, March, 1925. **643.** Frankolin, *E*, July, 1915. **644.** A, *E*, Oct., 1924. **645.** Swamp Angel, *C*, May 1, 1900. **646.** Chris, *E*, Aug., 1913. **647.** Rebus Myth, *AP*, Nov. 15, 1901. **648.** A, *C*, Dec. 15, 1911. **649.** un. **650.** Cincinnatus, *E*, Nov., 1925.

651. E. S. Crow, *C*, March 29, 1912. **652.** V. **653.** Kenneth, *EE*, Jan., 1903. **654.** EB, 1932. **655.** Palea, *Mystic Tree*, March, 1899. **656.** A, *E*, Dec., 1910. **657.** Q., *E*, Jan., 1921. **658.** HWB, in *Language on Vacation*, by D. A.

Borgmann, Scribner's, 1965. **659.** HWB, in *Language on Vacation*, by D. A. Borgmann, Scribner's, 1965. **660.** un. **661.** R. E. Reizenstein, Iowa City, 1935. **662.** E. S. Crow, *E*, March, 1914. **663.** Major Dome, *The Hermit and Crypt*, Aug., 1898. **664.** *Notes and Queries*, London, June 4, 1853. **665.** Byrnhec, *EE*, Dec., 1898. **666.** (a) un. (b) Jason, *AP*, Sept. 15, 1902. **667.** Walsh's *Handbook of Literary Curiosities*. **668.** Walsh's *Handbook of Literary Curiosities*. **669.** GBK, 1934. **670.** Jason, *AP*, July 1, 1906. **671.** Binks, *EE*, Dec., 1898. **672.** Tunste, *E*, Feb., 1918. **673.** Violet, *NP*, Aug. 18, 1907. **674.** Junius, *EE*, Dec., 1898. **675.** M, *E*, Nov., 1922.

676. Harry Ober, Brookline, Mass., 1935. **677.** Resolute, *E*, May, 1920. **678.** Vesta, *E*, Dec., 1919. **679.** DCV, *The Diamondalian*, May, 1897. **680.** M.C.S., *C*, Oct. 8, 1901. **681.** Spica, *C*, July 18, 1899. **682.** Stocles, *C*, April 26, 1898. **683.** Poly, *E*, Nov., 1917. **684.** George Clifton, Jr., Buffalo, N.Y., 1932. **685.** Leone, *Nutcracker's Corner*, Nov., 1897. **686.** Dorothy Doolittle, Holyoke *Transcript* puzzle column, Oct. 5, 1889. **687.** Alcyo, *Thedom*, April 15, 1889. **688.** un. **689.** Robert Hooke, Pittsburgh, 1934. **690.** Vesta, *E*, Jan., 1919. **691.** J. E. Reizenstein, Iowa City, 1934. **692.** N. Jineer, *E*, Aug., 1924. **693.** Gerald Lee Bergerson (age 11), 1968. **694.** After All, *Telegraph Twisters*, Aug., 1907. **695.** The Duke, *E*, June, 1913. **696.** Loris B. Curtis, Mason, Mich., 1935. **697.** Enavlicm, *E*, Nov., 1912. **698.** Nox, *Brighton Item*, Jan. 27, 1927. **699.** un. **700.** Bolis, *Golden Days*, Feb. 6, 1886.

701. DCV, *E*, Sept., 1919. **702.** O.W.L., *Mystic Laurels*, Oct. 11, 1885. **703.** P. O. Stage, *Golden Days*, Dec. 23, 1905. **704.** Pygmalion, *Golden Days*, Aug. 2, 1884. **705.** Atlantis, *E*, Sept., 1920. **706.** Arcanus, *C*, Jan. 11, 1905. **707.** David Shulman, New York, 1935. **708.** un. **709.** Moonshine, *E*, May, 1918. **710.** Arcanus, *NP*, March 30, 1907. **711.** King Carnival, *EE*, Dec., 1903. **712.** Captain Cuttle, *EE*, Dec., 1898. **713.** Tunste, *E*, Sept., 1924. **714.** Towhead, *E*, Jan., 1922. **715.** A, *E*, Aug., 1912. **716.** M. **717.** Cincinnatus, *AP*, June 15, 1899. **718.** Lord Elwood, *NP*, July 7, 1907. **719.** Chris, *E*, July, 1913. **720.** Rusticus, *AP*, Sept. 15, 1906. **721.** Author unknown, *Farmer's Almanac*, 1838. **722.** Francolin, *E*, July, 1915. **723.** Darryl H. Francis, Hounslow, Middlesex, England, *Word Ways*, Nov., 1968. **724.** A. **725.** Spud, *E*, Dec., 1923.

726. Sphinx, *The Study*, Dec. 25, 1890. **727.** Balmartelia, *Perplexities*, Feb. 24, 1900. **728.** Rosiemont, *AP*, July 15, 1902. **729.** All by Skeeziks, *Thedom*, July 24, 1889. **730.** Gi Gantic, *AP*, Oct. 15, 1908. **731.** E. S. Crow, *E*, May, 1912. **732.** Sphinx, *Oracle*, Feb., 1899. **733.** Major Dome, *The Hermit and Crypt*, Feb., 1898. **734.** DCV, *E*, March, 1920. **735.** Jack o' Lantern, *E*, June, 1924. **736.** Hercules. **737.** Ernest, *C*, Dec. 9, 1903. **738.** Atlantis, *E*, June, 1911. **739.** un. **740.** Arty Fishel, *The Study*, Oct. 22, 1886. **741.** Anonyme, *Mystic Retreat*, Aug., 1889. **742.** DCV, *EE*, Dec., 1898. **743.** A, *E*, June, 1913. **744.** Awl Wrong, *E*, April, 1926. **745.** V, *Geagua Leader*. **746.** Author unknown, *Farmer's Almanac*, 1812. **747.** GBK, 1936. **748.** *Enigmatic Oddities*, Nov. 27, 1903. **749.** un. **750.** Margaretta, *C*, July 4, 1906.

751. Frankolin, *E*, April, 1915. **752.** R. O. Chester, *NP*, Jan. 7, 1905. **753.** A, *Enigmatic Oddities*, Nov. 10, 1901. **754.** Sphinx, *Puzzle Calls*, Jan. 26, 1889. **755.** Anonyme, *E*, Dec., 1913. **756.** Verdant Green, *EE*, Dec., 1898. **757.** Chris, *E*, Feb., 1915. **758.** (a) un. (b) HWB. **759.** A, *E*, Feb., 1911. **760.** Martella, *Perplexities*, Oct. 20, 1900. **761.** (a) Dr. Arthur Kleykamp, St. Louis, 1932. (b) Chris, *E*, Nov., 1914. **762.** GBK, 1934. **763.** DCV, *Golden Days*, July 14, 1897. **764.** un. **765.** Kee Pon, *E*, Dec., 1923. **766.** Sphinx, *C*, Sept. 13, 1898. **767.** un. **768.** After All, *AP*, Sept. 15, 1906. **769.** Atlantis, *E*, Feb., 1915. **770.** The Gopher, *NP*, July 9, 1905. **771.** L'Allegro, *Mystic Tree*, Nov., 1900. **772.** Kenneth, *C*, Nov. 27, 1900. **773.** A, *E*, July, 1925. **774.** (a) un. (b) Lord Baltimore, *Oracle*, Feb., 1891. **775.** Dorothy Doolittle, *AP*, March 1, 1908.

776. N. Jineer, *E*, Aug., 1923. **777.** Vesta, *E*, Aug., 1919. **778.** Balmar, *C*, Dec. 18, 1900. **779.** Gi Gantic, *AP*, Oct. 15, 1908. **780.** Mabel P., *C*, June 20, 1899. **781.** Miss T. Ree, *Arcana*, May, 1887. **782.** Osceola, *Golden Days*, Sept. 23, 1899. **783.** M.C.S., *C*, Dec. 26, 1899. **784.** Balmar, *Perplexities*, April 7, 1900. **785.** Jemand, *E*, July, 1926. **786.** Enavlicm, *E*, April, 1918. **787.** Quidam, *Telegraph Twisters*, April, 1905. **788.** Ellsworth. **789.** Lord Baltimore, *Mystery*, May 7, 1896. **790.** Nelsonian, *Mystic Tree*, Aug. 18, 1887. **791.** H. B. McPherrin, Denver, 1932. **792.** A, *C*, Jan. 13, 1911. **793.** un. **794.** Miss Anna C. Bardnell, Canaserage, N.Y., 1932. **795.** un. **796.** Arty Ess, *E*, April, 1913. **797.** EB, 1932. **798.** DCV, *Perplexities*, Aug. 11, 1900. **799.** A. F. Holt, *C*, March 28, 1897. **800.** Chester A. Griffin, Franklin, N.H., 1934.

801. (a) Violet, *NP*, Aug. 25, 1906. (b) A, *E*, Dec., 1910. **802.** E. S. Crow, *E*, May, 1917. **803.** Hera and Zeus, *Mystic Dots*, Jan., 1899. **804.** DCV, *E*, May, 1919. **805.** M, *AP*, Oct. 15, 1906. **806.** Gentle Annie, *Mystic Argosy*, May 26, 1900. **807.** Rhoda, *E*, Sept., 1920. **808.** un. **809.** Moonshine, *E*, Sept., 1916. **810.** N. Jineer, *E*, May, 1925. **811.** Mrs. Bernice Loidl, Stillwater, N.Y., 1933. **812.** Enavlicm, *E*, May, 1921. **813.** Josepha Byrne Heifitz, *Word Ways*, May, 1970. **814.** O. R. Egon, *AP*, Sept. 9, 1899. **815.** HWB. **816.** Sam Slick, *E*, Dec., 1916. **817.** Fred Domino, *E*, Dec., 1923. **818.** Delian, *C*, Aug. 7, 1900. **819.** W. E. Stern, *E*, Aug., 1921. **820.** Francolin, *E*, Jan., 1915. **821.** M. O. Wellman, Lansing, Mich., 1932. **822.** D.C.V, *AP*, Sept. 15, 1907. **823.** un. **824.** Hercules, *E*, May, 1924. **825.** Hercules, *E*, Sept., 1924.

826. Authorship uncertain, *The Eurekan*, Feb., 1903. **827.** (a) Jack O' Lantern, *Golden Days*, April 20, 1889. (b) un. **828.** un. **829.** Gee, *E*, June, 1916. **830.** Ralph, *NP*, Nov., 1903. **831.** Balmar, *Mystic Argosy*, July 28, 1900. **832.** Percy Vere, *Puzzler's Gazette*, Nov. 30, 1890. **833.** Margaretta, *AP*, Jan. 1, 1901. **834.** Mazy Masker, *C*, Aug. 8, 1897. **835.** A, *Oracle*, March, 1906. **836.** Nelsonian, *C*, Feb. 13, 1907. **837.** M, *E*, Sept., 1923. **838.** M.C.S., *C*, Aug. 24, 1904. **839.** un. **840.** Ralph, *AP*, July 1, 1906. **841.** Hercules, *E*, July, 1924. **842.** M, *E*, May, 1925. **843.** A, *C*, Jan. 13, 1913. **844.** Jemand, *E*, June, 1919. **845.** Delian Band, *C*, Oct. 17, 1899. **846.** Nestor, *The Key*, July, 1891. **847.** Kenneth. **848.** Teepeekay, *Mysteriarchy*, Jan. 2, 1896. **849.** R, *E*, Dec., 1922. **850.** Orion, *E*, Sept., 1924.

851. A, *E*, Dec., 1910. **852.** Ess Ell, *C*, Sept. 4, 1908. **853.** A, *E*, March, 1924. **854.** R, *NP*, Aug. 25, 1907. **855.** Will I. Am, *NP*, April 28, 1906. **856.** M, *E*, Feb., 1915. **857.** A, *E*, March, 1918. **858.** EB, 1932. **859.** A.L.S., *AP*, July 15, 1905. **860.** M, *E*, Sept., 1921. **861.** R, *E*, April, 1912. **862.** Cincinnatus, *AP*, Dec. 2, 1899. **863.** M.C.S., *C*, Aug. 5, 1902. **864.** Wanderoo, *E*, Feb., 1913. **865.** Vesta, *E*, Nov., 1920. **866.** Ernest, *C*, Oct. 7, 1903. **867.** Balmar, *AP*, May 26, 1900. **868.** A, *E*, Jan., 1914. **869.** Mrs. John Matthews, Lenox, Mass., 1935. **870.** un. **871.** Hercules, *C*, 1894. **872.** Eruditus, *The Study*, Feb. 15, 1890. **873.** Anonyme, *The Oracle*, March 31, 1896. **874.** un. **875.** Bolis, *EE*, Dec., 1898.

876. Arty Ess, *E*, July, 1922. **877.** Rosiemont, *Marion Maze*, Jan. 5, 1899. **878.** Nox, *The Brighton Item*, March, 1914. **879.** A, *E*, April, 1925. **880.** M, *AP*, June 1, 1906. **881.** un. **882.** Jemand. **883.** Enavlicm, *E*, April, 1925. **884.** Al T. Tude, *E*, Feb., 1925. **885.** C. Saw, *Perplexities*, Feb. 18, 1898. **886.** Bolis, *Key to Puzzledom*, 1906. **887.** M, *B&O Magazine*, Nov., 1925. **888.** Koscisuko McGinty, *AP*, Dec. 1, 1904. **889.** V. **890.** Jemand, *E*, May, 1913. **891.** Hercules, *E*. **892.** A, *E*, May, 1925. **893.** Beech Nut, *Perplexities*, Dec. 12, 1889. **894.** Alec Sander, *E*, April, 1918. **895.** Enavlicm, *E*, Jan., 1917. **896.** (a) A.

(b) Josepha Byrne Heifitz, *Word Ways*, May, 1970. **897.** Johank, *AP*, March 15, 1902. **898.** V. I. King, *C*, Nov. 25, 1903. **899.** A, *Enigmatic Oddities*, June 30, 1901. **900.** C. L. Oser, *E*, March, 1917. **901.** DCV, *C*, Aug. 28, 1900. **902.** King Carnival, *Golden Days*, 1898. **903.** Ed Ward, *E*, June, 1915. **904.** A, *E*, Nov., 1912. **905.** Will I. Am, *NP*, May 19, 1906. **906.** Nypho, *E*, Dec., 1925. **907.** un. **908.** R, *E*, March, 1925. **909.** Atlantis, *AP*, Aug. 1, 1925. **910.** Vesta, *E*, July, 1920. **911.** DCV, *Golden Days*, Oct. 28, 1897. **912.** (a) Jim C. Rack, *Our Deep Perplexities*, Aug., 1888. (b) A, *The Oracle*, Dec. 15, 1911. **913.** R, *E*, July, 1915. **914.** Ace, *Mystic Argosy*, Feb. 5, 1898. **915.** After All, *NP*, Dec. 29, 1906. **916.** A. **917.** (a) A. (b) V, *E*. **918.** A. **919.** (a) un. (b) Robert Hooke, Pittsburgh, 1934. **920.** (a) M, *E*, Dec., 1920. (b) V, *E*. **921.** V, *E*. **922.** W. Upp, *EE*, Dec., 1898. **923.** A, *E*, July, 1913. **924.** Balmar, *C*, June 19, 1900. **925.** The Gopher, *NP*, Aug. 13, 1905. **926.** un. **927.** un. **928.** Joaquin, *Mystic Argosy*, Feb. 26, 1898. **929.** Minnie Mum, *E*, July, 1924. **930.** Sans Souci, *EE*, Dec., 1898. **931.** H. I. Story, *Golden Days*, Jan. 5, 1889. **932.** Enavlicm, *E*, June, 1924. **933.** Ed Ward, *AP*, June 15, 1903. **934.** Blackbird, *AP*, April 15, 1903. **935.** Barnyard, *E*, Oct., 1917. **936.** A, *E*, July, 1925. **937.** Enavlicm, *Enigmatic Oddities*, 1906. **938.** Q., *E*, Aug., 1911. **939.** M.C.S., *Mystery*, Oct. 12, 1893. **940.** un. **941.** Jemand, *E*, Nov., 1925. **942.** Gem, *E*, Feb., 1915. **943.** A, *E*, June, 1917. **944.** Rhoda, *E*, Jan., 1921. **945.** Moonshine, *E*, Jan., 1916. **946.** Nypho. **947.** Kenneth, *Perplexities*, Jan. 25, 1899. **948.** Balmar, *E*, April, 1910. **949.** Arty Ess, *C*, June 19, 1908. **950.** A, *E*, April, 1924. **951.** A, *Oracle*, Sept., 1906. **952.** Osaple, *E*, Aug., 1925. **953.** Both by Nypho, *E*, Feb., 1900. **954.** (a) Sphinx, *C*, Aug. 15, 1899. (b) R, *E*, Oct., 1917. **955.** England, *EE*, Dec., 1898. **956.** C.A.H., *C*, Aug. 4, 1911. **957.** un. **958.** Mystery, *E*, June, 1920. **959.** Walsh's *Handbook of Literary Curiosities*, 1892. **960.** Anonyme, *E*, Dec., 1922. **961.** Frankolin, *E*, Sept., 1915. **962.** Fred Domino, *AP*, May, 1909. **963.** P. O. Stage, *Mystic Tree*, June, 1898. **964.** (a) Dr. Fred L. Story, Ennis, Texas, 1936. (b) Kenneth, *E*, Sept., 1924. **965.** V, *E*. **966.** R, *E*, May, 1913. **967.** A. **968.** Remlap, *Marion Maze*, Nov. 18, 1898. **969.** *Notes and Queries*, June 4, 1853. **970.** (a) Wheatley's *Anagrams*, London, 1862. (b) Guidon, *AP*, March 16, 1901. **971.** (a) Q., *E*, Oct., 1910. (b) E. S. Crow, *E*, Nov., 1910. **972.** R, *Brighton Item*, Oct. 14, 1911. **973.** A, *E*, Oct., 1910. **974.** Q., *E*, Oct., 1912. **975.** Poly, *The Black Imp*, Oct., 1897. **976.** Sam Slick, *E*, Oct., 1914. **977.** Francoline, *E*, Dec., 1915. **978.** V, *E*. **979.** Evening Star, *The Mystic Promoter*. **980.** PJF, 1935. **981.** Arcanus, *C*, March 12, 1909. **982.** DCV, *Golden Days*, June 20, 1897. **983.** Nelsonian, *Puzzlemaze*, April 6, 1887. **984.** Abel Em, *NP*, d.u. **985.** Joe Mullins, *E*, June, 1924. **986.** Atlas, *B&O Magazine*, May, 1926. **987.** Alec Sander, *Telegraph Twisters*, Jan. 1, 1906. **988.** R, *E*, March, 1917. **989.** M.C.S., *C*, Feb. 7, 1907. **990.** Justa Parson, *Oracle*, May, 1897. **991.** Rex, *AP*, Jan. 1, 1901. **992.** Jemand. **993.** (a) Rusticus, *AP*, Sept. 15, 1906. (b) Jemand, *E*, Aug., 1923. **994.** T.H., *Enigmatic Oddities*, June 9, 1901. **995.** E. S. Crow, *E*, Jan., 1914. **996.** Hercules, *E*, Dec., 1925. **997.** Hercules, *E*. **998.** Spica, *C*, Feb. 8, 1905. **999.** A, *E*, April, 1924. **1000.** A, *C*, April 7, 1911.

1001. All five by Skeeziks, *Thedom*, June 15, 1895. **1002.** (a) Primrose, *EE*, Dec., 1903. (b) DCV, *AP*, March 15, 1908. **1003.** Atlantis, *E*, Feb., 1911. **1004.** un. **1005.** T.H., *Enigmatic Oddities*, Feb. 23, 1902. **1006.** A, *E*, Nov., 1925. **1007.** Horation, *E*, Feb., 1919. **1008.** Walsh's *Handbook of Literary Curiosities*, 1862. **1009.** E. S. Crow, *E*, Feb., 1911. **1010.** Joe, *Geagua Leader*. **1011.** R, *C*, April 30, 1909. **1012.** Margaretta, *E*, Aug., 1922. **1013.** Johank,

AP, Sept. 1, 1901. **1014.** Francolin, *E*, April, 1915. **1015.** George C. Lamb, Burton, Ohio, 1935. **1016.** C. Saw, *Puzzleland*, May, 1899. **1017.** un. **1018.** Arcanus, *E*, April, 1914. **1019.** DCV, *C*, April 28, 1903. **1020.** Francolin, *E*, Sept., 1914. **1021.** Gwendoline, *C*, Aug. 2, 1912. **1022.** M.C.S., *Enigmatic Oddities*, Feb. 12, 1905. **1023.** Francolin, *E*, March, 1916. **1024.** un. **1025.** Francolin, *AP*, July 1, 1905. **1026.** un. **1027.** Frans Folks, *Enigmatic Oddities*, Nov. 27, 1903. **1028.** (a) Comrade, *Oracle*, Dec., 1896. (b) Hercules, Dec., 1896. **1029.** (a) Jason, *E*, April, 1910. (b) R, *E*, Dec., 1919. **1030.** Jason, *AP*, March, 1901. **1031.** C.A.H., *C*, Dec. 22, 1911. **1032.** Asian, *Mystery*, Nov. 19, 1891. **1033.** PJF, 1935. **1034.** Jamaica, *NP*, Aug. 20, 1905. **1035.** Bolis, *Golden Days*, Aug. 1, 1885. **1036.** De. Ralf, *Golden Days*, Oct. 25, 1884. **1037.** Darryl H. Francis, Hounslow, Middlesex, England, *Word Ways*, Nov., 1968. **1038.** A, *E*, Aug., 1925. **1039.** DCV, *NP*, Aug. 4, 1906. **1040.** Henry D. Howell, Middleton, Del., 1932. **1041.** A, *E*, Aug., 1926. **1042.** Nestor, *Thedom*, Feb. 25, 1890. **1043.** Lew Ward, *Golden Days*, Aug. 27, 1887. **1044.** Rusticus, *AP*, May 15, 1908. **1045.** Rex Ford, *Golden Days*, June 24, 1899. **1046.** Gee, *E*, Aug., 1913. **1047.** A, *E*, March, 1917. **1048.** A, *Enigmatic Oddities*, Aug. 11, 1901. **1049.** Evening Star, *AP*, July 15, 1906. **1050.** DCV, *Golden Days*, July 28, 1897.

1051. Nox, *Brighton Item*, June 2, 1917. **1052.** Arcanus, *AP*, May 1, 1908. **1053.** La Noitan, *E*, Nov., 1913. **1054.** EB, 1934. **1055.** Myself, *NP*, July 13, 1908. **1056.** Avocania, *Perplexities*, May 26, 1900. **1057.** Gwendoline, *Thedom*, May, 1894. **1058.** A, *E*, Feb., 1911. **1059.** Wanderoo, *E*, Jan., 1918. **1060.** R, *E*, Feb., 1918. **1061.** Pygmalion, *Golden Days*, Nov. 6, 1896. **1062.** A, *E*, Nov., 1925. **1063.** Moonshine, *E*, Aug., 1920. **1064.** (a) C. Saw, *Mystery*, May 28, 1896. (b) A, *E*, June, 1926. **1065.** Mrs. John Matthews, Lenox, Mass., 1935. **1066.** Nelsonian, *EE*, Dec., 1898. **1067.** DCV, *E*, Jan., 1918. **1068.** E. L. Benfer, Fair Haven, N.J., 1933. **1069.** un. **1070.** Primrose, *AP*, May 6, 1899. **1071.** Primrose, *E*, April, 1925. **1072.** Bolis, *EE*, Dec., 1898. **1073.** Noble Holderread, Milford, Ind., 1933. **1074.** Balmar, *AP*, Dec. 2, 1899. **1075.** Musicus, *NP*.

1076. Mam, *E*, Dec., 1923. **1077.** Sam Slick, *E*, April, 1915. **1078.** Arty Ess, *E*, Jan., 1922. **1079.** Alcyo, *E*, March, 1926. **1080.** Jack O' Lantern, *The Key*, Nov., 1891. **1081.** Balmar, *AP*, Dec. 2, 1899. **1082.** un. **1083.** (a, b, c) All three from Walsh's *Handbook of Literary Curiosities*, 1892. (d) Wah-ta-Wah, *Golden Days*, Nov. 3, 1898. **1084.** Remlap, *EE*, Dec., 1898. **1085.** Minnie Mum, *E*, July, 1925. **1086.** Jason, *Perplexities*, Dec. 8, 1900. **1087.** V, *E*. **1088.** (a) Frans Faolks, *AP*, Oct. 15, 1902. (b) A, *E*, Nov., 1925. (c) Hercules, *E*. (d) Author uncertain, *AP*, Oct. 15, 1902. **1089.** E. S. Crow, *E*, Dec., 1925. **1090.** M, *E*, Dec., 1925. **1091.** A, *E*, Dec., 1924. **1092.** Nypho, *E*, July, 1920. **1093.** P. Chinn, *In Mystic Mood*, June, 1911. **1094.** Q., *E*, April, 1920. **1095.** Envalicm, *E*, May, 1926. **1096.** Authorship uncertain, *Golden Days*, May 16, 1885. **1097.** M.C.S., *Mysteries*, Dec. 7, 1893. **1098.** Margaretta, *E*, Nov., 1922. **1099.** Ed Ward, *E*, May, 1915. **1100.** un.

1101. Kenneth, *EE*, Dec., 1903. **1102.** un. **1103.** A, *E*, March, 1918. **1104.** Darryl H. Francis, Hounslow, Middlesex, England, *Word Ways*, Nov., 1968. **1105.** Skeeziks, *Thedom*, April 15, 1889. **1106.** E. S. Crow, *E*, Aug., 1910. **1107.** Two Johns, *EE*, Dec., 1903. **1108.** Nestor, *EE*, Dec., 1898. **1109.** C. Saw, *E*, Nov. 11, 1911. **1110.** Ed Ward, *E*, June, 1915. **1111.** Tranza, *Oracle*, Oct., 1906. **1112.** Nelsonian, *The Mystic Art*, Jan. 19, 1888. **1113.** Hercules, *E*. **1114.** A, *E*, May, 1920. **1115.** Tranza, *C*, Jan. 2, 1900. **1116.** Moonshine, *E*, June, 1917. **1117.** Walsh's *Handbook of Literary Curiosities*, 1892. **1118.** Francoline, *E*, Aug., 1915. **1119.** un. **1120.** Nelsonian, *The Study*, May 6, 1887.

1121. Sub Rosa, *The Labyrinth*, May 1, 1887. **1122.** un. **1123.** (a) HWB. (b) DAB; both first published in *Language on Vacation*, by D. A. Borgmann. **1124.** A, *E*, Feb., 1926. **1125.** R, *NP*, Dec., 1909. **1126.** Sir Vare, *E*, Feb., 1921. **1127.** Nox, *Brighton Item*, Sept. 18, 1915. **1128.** M, *C*, July 10, 1907. **1129.** Margaretta, *AP*, March 3, 1900. **1130.** Am I. Right, *E*, June, 1921. **1131.** Resolute, *AP*, Nov. 15, 1905. **1132.** Donatello, *E*, July, 1913. **1133.** Tyron, *E*, July, 1914. **1134.** (a) A, *C*, July 20, 1904. (b) V, *E*. **1135.** Enavlicm, *E*, June, 1923. **1136.** un. **1137.** V. **1138.** E. S. Crow, *E*, March, 1913. **1139.** Peanuts, *EE*, Dec., 1898. **1140.** Phil Down, *AP*, July 13, 1901. **1141.** Jo Mullins, *E*, Oct. 10, 1920. **1142.** (a) Trux Specs, *EE*, Dec., 1898. (b) R, *E*, April, 1926. **1143.** (a) Skeeziks, *Thedom*, Nov. 10, 1890. (b) Hercules. **1144.** A, *B&O Magazine*, March, 1925. **1146.** E. S. Crow, *E*, June, 1920. **1145.** Anonyme, *E*, Jan., 1914. **1147.** R, *E*, April, 1926. **1148.** Darryl H. Francis, Hounslow, Middlesex, England, *Word Ways*, Nov., 1968. **1149.** Meteor, *EE*, Dec., 1898. **1150.** DCV, *E*, April, 1913. **1151.** Q., *AP*, May 15, 1907. **1152.** Le Dare, *E*, Feb., 1922. **1153.** un. **1154.** A, *E*, June, 1925. **1155.** Topay, *Nonplustics*, 1896. **1156.** Arcanus, *Oracle*, June, 1907. **1157.** Sol, *E*, July, 1926. **1158.** R, *E*, Jan., 1926. **1159.** A, *E*, July, 1925. **1160.** R, *E*, Sept., 1918. **1161.** R, *E*, March, 1917. **1162.** (a, b) Lewis Carroll. (b–e) The second through the fifth anagrams are from *The Modern Sphinx*, June, 1879. (f, g) Sixth and seventh are from Wheatley's *Anagrams*, London, 1862. (h) Lei Pziger, *Golden Days*, March 6, 1886. **1163.** Balmar, *C*, Sept. 2, 1910. **1164.** Sphinx, *C*, Oct. 9, 1908. **1165.** (a) Primrose, *The Mystic Era*, 1896. (b) M.C.S., *C*, June 9, 1908. **1166.** DCV, *Mystic Dots*, Jan., 1899. **1167.** un. **1168.** un. **1169.** un.

A CATALOGUE OF SELECTED DOVER BOOKS
IN ALL FIELDS OF INTEREST

A CATALOGUE OF SELECTED DOVER BOOKS
IN ALL FIELDS OF INTEREST

AMERICA'S OLD MASTERS, James T. Flexner. Four men emerged unexpectedly from provincial 18th century America to leadership in European art: Benjamin West, J. S. Copley, C. R. Peale, Gilbert Stuart. Brilliant coverage of lives and contributions. Revised, 1967 edition. 69 plates. 365pp. of text.

21806-6 Paperbound $3.00

FIRST FLOWERS OF OUR WILDERNESS: AMERICAN PAINTING, THE COLONIAL PERIOD, James T. Flexner. Painters, and regional painting traditions from earliest Colonial times up to the emergence of Copley, West and Peale Sr., Foster, Gustavus Hesselius, Feke, John Smibert and many anonymous painters in the primitive manner. Engaging presentation, with 162 illustrations. xxii + 368pp.

22180-6 Paperbound $3.50

THE LIGHT OF DISTANT SKIES: AMERICAN PAINTING, 1760-1835, James T. Flexner. The great generation of early American painters goes to Europe to learn and to teach: West, Copley, Gilbert Stuart and others. Allston, Trumbull, Morse; also contemporary American painters—primitives, derivatives, academics—who remained in America. 102 illustrations. xiii + 306pp.

22179-2 Paperbound $3.00

A HISTORY OF THE RISE AND PROGRESS OF THE ARTS OF DESIGN IN THE UNITED STATES, William Dunlap. Much the richest mine of information on early American painters, sculptors, architects, engravers, miniaturists, etc. The only source of information for scores of artists, the major primary source for many others. Unabridged reprint of rare original 1834 edition, with new introduction by James T. Flexner, and 394 new illustrations. Edited by Rita Weiss. 6⅝ x 9⅝.

21695-0, 21696-9, 21697-7 Three volumes, Paperbound $13.50

EPOCHS OF CHINESE AND JAPANESE ART, Ernest F. Fenollosa. From primitive Chinese art to the 20th century, thorough history, explanation of every important art period and form, including Japanese woodcuts; main stress on China and Japan, but Tibet, Korea also included. Still unexcelled for its detailed, rich coverage of cultural background, aesthetic elements, diffusion studies, particularly of the historical period. 2nd, 1913 edition. 242 illustrations. lii + 439pp. of text.

20364-6, 20365-4 Two volumes, Paperbound $6.00

THE GENTLE ART OF MAKING ENEMIES, James A. M. Whistler. Greatest wit of his day deflates Oscar Wilde, Ruskin, Swinburne; strikes back at inane critics, exhibitions, art journalism; aesthetics of impressionist revolution in most striking form. Highly readable classic by great painter. Reproduction of edition designed by Whistler. Introduction by Alfred Werner. xxxvi + 334pp.

21875-9 Paperbound $2.50

CATALOGUE OF DOVER BOOKS

VISUAL ILLUSIONS: THEIR CAUSES, CHARACTERISTICS, AND APPLICATIONS, Matthew Luckiesh. Thorough description and discussion of optical illusion, geometric and perspective, particularly; size and shape distortions, illusions of color, of motion; natural illusions; use of illusion in art and magic, industry, etc. Most useful today with op art, also for classical art. Scores of effects illustrated. Introduction by William H. Ittleson. 100 illustrations. xxi + 252pp.
21530-X Paperbound $2.00

A HANDBOOK OF ANATOMY FOR ART STUDENTS, Arthur Thomson. Thorough, virtually exhaustive coverage of skeletal structure, musculature, etc. Full text, supplemented by anatomical diagrams and drawings and by photographs of undraped figures. Unique in its comparison of male and female forms, pointing out differences of contour, texture, form. 211 figures, 40 drawings, 86 photographs. xx + 459pp. 5⅜ x 8⅜.
21163-0 Paperbound $3.50

150 MASTERPIECES OF DRAWING, Selected by Anthony Toney. Full page reproductions of drawings from the early 16th to the end of the 18th century, all beautifully reproduced: Rembrandt, Michelangelo, Dürer, Fragonard, Urs, Graf, Wouwerman, many others. First-rate browsing book, model book for artists. xviii + 150pp. 8⅜ x 11¼.
21032-4 Paperbound $2.50

THE LATER WORK OF AUBREY BEARDSLEY, Aubrey Beardsley. Exotic, erotic, ironic masterpieces in full maturity: Comedy Ballet, Venus and Tannhauser, Pierrot, Lysistrata, Rape of the Lock, Savoy material, Ali Baba, Volpone, etc. This material revolutionized the art world, and is still powerful, fresh, brilliant. With *The Early Work,* all Beardsley's finest work. 174 plates, 2 in color. xiv + 176pp. 8⅛ x 11.
21817-1 Paperbound $3.00

DRAWINGS OF REMBRANDT, Rembrandt van Rijn. Complete reproduction of fabulously rare edition by Lippmann and Hofstede de Groot, completely reedited, updated, improved by Prof. Seymour Slive, Fogg Museum. Portraits, Biblical sketches, landscapes, Oriental types, nudes, episodes from classical mythology—All Rembrandt's fertile genius. Also selection of drawings by his pupils and followers. "Stunning volumes," *Saturday Review.* 550 illustrations. lxxviii + 552pp. 9⅛ x 12¼.
21485-0, 21486-9 Two volumes, Paperbound $10.00

THE DISASTERS OF WAR, Francisco Goya. One of the masterpieces of Western civilization—83 etchings that record Goya's shattering, bitter reaction to the Napoleonic war that swept through Spain after the insurrection of 1808 and to war in general. Reprint of the first edition, with three additional plates from Boston's Museum of Fine Arts. All plates facsimile size. Introduction by Philip Hofer, Fogg Museum. v + 97pp. 9⅜ x 8¼.
21872-4 Paperbound $2.00

GRAPHIC WORKS OF ODILON REDON. Largest collection of Redon's graphic works ever assembled: 172 lithographs, 28 etchings and engravings, 9 drawings. These include some of his most famous works. All the plates from *Odilon Redon: oeuvre graphique complet,* plus additional plates. New introduction and caption translations by Alfred Werner. 209 illustrations. xxvii + 209pp. 9⅛ x 12¼.
21966-8 Paperbound $4.00

DESIGN BY ACCIDENT; A BOOK OF "ACCIDENTAL EFFECTS" FOR ARTISTS AND
DESIGNERS, James F. O'Brien. Create your own unique, striking, imaginative effects
by "controlled accident" interaction of materials: paints and lacquers, oil and water
based paints, splatter, crackling materials, shatter, similar items. Everything you do
will be different; first book on this limitless art, so useful to both fine artist and
commercial artist. Full instructions. 192 plates showing "accidents," 8 in color.
viii + 215pp. 8⅜ x 11¼. 21942-9 Paperbound $3.50

THE BOOK OF SIGNS, Rudolf Koch. Famed German type designer draws 493 beautiful symbols: religious, mystical, alchemical, imperial, property marks, runes, etc.
Remarkable fusion of traditional and modern. Good for suggestions of timelessness,
smartness, modernity. Text. vi + 104pp. 6⅛ x 9¼.
20162-7 Paperbound $1.25

HISTORY OF INDIAN AND INDONESIAN ART, Ananda K. Coomaraswamy. An unabridged republication of one of the finest books by a great scholar in Eastern art.
Rich in descriptive material, history, social backgrounds; Sunga reliefs, Rajput
paintings, Gupta temples, Burmese frescoes, textiles, jewelry, sculpture, etc. 400
photos. viii + 423pp. 6⅜ x 9¾. 21436-2 Paperbound $4.00

PRIMITIVE ART, Franz Boas. America's foremost anthropologist surveys textiles,
ceramics, woodcarving, basketry, metalwork, etc.; patterns, technology, creation of
symbols, style origins. All areas of world, but very full on Northwest Coast Indians.
More than 350 illustrations of baskets, boxes, totem poles, weapons, etc. 378 pp.
20025-6 Paperbound $3.00

THE GENTLEMAN AND CABINET MAKER'S DIRECTOR, Thomas Chippendale. Full
reprint (third edition, 1762) of most influential furniture book of all time, by
master cabinetmaker. 200 plates, illustrating chairs, sofas, mirrors, tables, cabinets,
plus 24 photographs of surviving pieces. Biographical introduction by N. Bienen-
stock. vi + 249pp. 9⅞ x 12¾. 21601-2 Paperbound $4.00

AMERICAN ANTIQUE FURNITURE, Edgar G. Miller, Jr. The basic coverage of all
American furniture before 1840. Individual chapters cover type of furniture—
clocks, tables, sideboards, etc.—chronologically, with inexhaustible wealth of data.
More than 2100 photographs, all identified, commented on. Essential to all early
American collectors. Introduction by H. E. Keyes. vi + 1106pp. 7⅞ x 10¾.
21599-7, 21600-4 Two volumes, Paperbound $11.00

PENNSYLVANIA DUTCH AMERICAN FOLK ART, Henry J. Kauffman. 279 photos,
28 drawings of tulipware, Fraktur script, painted tinware, toys, flowered furniture,
quilts, samplers, hex signs, house interiors, etc. Full descriptive text. Excellent for
tourist, rewarding for designer, collector. Map. 146pp. 7⅞ x 10¾.
21205-X Paperbound $2.50

EARLY NEW ENGLAND GRAVESTONE RUBBINGS, Edmund V. Gillon, Jr. 43 photographs, 226 carefully reproduced rubbings show heavily symbolic, sometimes
macabre early gravestones, up to early 19th century. Remarkable early American
primitive art, occasionally strikingly beautiful; always powerful. Text. xxvi +
207pp. 8⅜ x 11¼. 21380-3 Paperbound $3.50

ALPHABETS AND ORNAMENTS, Ernst Lehner. Well-known pictorial source for decorative alphabets, script examples, cartouches, frames, decorative title pages, calligraphic initials, borders, similar material. 14th to 19th century, mostly European. Useful in almost any graphic arts designing, varied styles. 750 illustrations. 256pp. 7 x 10.   21905-4 Paperbound $4.00

PAINTING: A CREATIVE APPROACH, Norman Colquhoun. For the beginner simple guide provides an instructive approach to painting: major stumbling blocks for beginner; overcoming them, technical points; paints and pigments; oil painting; watercolor and other media and color. New section on "plastic" paints. Glossary. Formerly *Paint Your Own Pictures*. 221pp.   22000-1 Paperbound $1.75

THE ENJOYMENT AND USE OF COLOR, Walter Sargent. Explanation of the relations between colors themselves and between colors in nature and art, including hundreds of little-known facts about color values, intensities, effects of high and low illumination, complementary colors. Many practical hints for painters, references to great masters. 7 color plates, 29 illustrations. x + 274pp.
20944-X Paperbound $2.75

THE NOTEBOOKS OF LEONARDO DA VINCI, compiled and edited by Jean Paul Richter. 1566 extracts from original manuscripts reveal the full range of Leonardo's versatile genius: all his writings on painting, sculpture, architecture, anatomy, astronomy, geography, topography, physiology, mining, music, etc., in both Italian and English, with 186 plates of manuscript pages and more than 500 additional drawings. Includes studies for the Last Supper, the lost Sforza monument, and other works. Total of xlvii + 866pp. 7⅞ x 10¾.
22572-0, 22573-9 Two volumes, Paperbound $10.00

MONTGOMERY WARD CATALOGUE OF 1895. Tea gowns, yards of flannel and pillow-case lace, stereoscopes, books of gospel hymns, the New Improved Singer Sewing Machine, side saddles, milk skimmers, straight-edged razors, high-button shoes, spittoons, and on and on . . . listing some 25,000 items, practically all illustrated. Essential to the shoppers of the 1890's, it is our truest record of the spirit of the period. Unaltered reprint of Issue No. 57, Spring and Summer 1895. Introduction by Boris Emmet. Innumerable illustrations. xiii + 624pp. 8½ x 11⅝.
22377-9 Paperbound $6.95

THE CRYSTAL PALACE EXHIBITION ILLUSTRATED CATALOGUE (LONDON, 1851). One of the wonders of the modern world—the Crystal Palace Exhibition in which all the nations of the civilized world exhibited their achievements in the arts and sciences—presented in an equally important illustrated catalogue. More than 1700 items pictured with accompanying text—ceramics, textiles, cast-iron work, carpets, pianos, sleds, razors, wall-papers, billiard tables, beehives, silverware and hundreds of other artifacts—represent the focal point of Victorian culture in the Western World. Probably the largest collection of Victorian decorative art ever assembled— indispensable for antiquarians and designers. Unabridged republication of the Art-Journal Catalogue of the Great Exhibition of 1851, with all terminal essays. New introduction by John Gloag, F.S.A. xxxiv + 426pp. 9 x 12.
22503-8 Paperbound $4.50

A History of Costume, Carl Köhler. Definitive history, based on surviving pieces of clothing primarily, and paintings, statues, etc. secondarily. Highly readable text, supplemented by 594 illustrations of costumes of the ancient Mediterranean peoples, Greece and Rome, the Teutonic prehistoric period; costumes of the Middle Ages, Renaissance, Baroque, 18th and 19th centuries. Clear, measured patterns are provided for many clothing articles. Approach is practical throughout. Enlarged by Emma von Sichart. 464pp.   21030-8 Paperbound $3.50

Oriental Rugs, Antique and Modern, Walter A. Hawley. A complete and authoritative treatise on the Oriental rug—where they are made, by whom and how, designs and symbols, characteristics in detail of the six major groups, how to distinguish them and how to buy them. Detailed technical data is provided on periods, weaves, warps, wefts, textures, sides, ends and knots, although no technical background is required for an understanding. 11 color plates, 80 halftones, 4 maps. vi + 320pp. 6⅛ x 9⅛.   22366-3 Paperbound $5.00

Ten Books on Architecture, Vitruvius. By any standards the most important book on architecture ever written. Early Roman discussion of aesthetics of building, construction methods, orders, sites, and every other aspect of architecture has inspired, instructed architecture for about 2,000 years. Stands behind Palladio, Michelangelo, Bramante, Wren, countless others. Definitive Morris H. Morgan translation. 68 illustrations. xii + 331pp.   20645-9 Paperbound $3.50

The Four Books of Architecture, Andrea Palladio. Translated into every major Western European language in the two centuries following its publication in 1570, this has been one of the most influential books in the history of architecture. Complete reprint of the 1738 Isaac Ware edition. New introduction by Adolf Placzek, Columbia Univ. 216 plates. xxii + 110pp. of text. 9½ x 12¾.
21308-0 Clothbound $10.00

Sticks and Stones: A Study of American Architecture and Civilization, Lewis Mumford. One of the great classics of American cultural history. American architecture from the medieval-inspired earliest forms to the early 20th century; evolution of structure and style, and reciprocal influences on environment. 21 photographic illustrations. 238pp.   20202-X Paperbound $2.00

The American Builder's Companion, Asher Benjamin. The most widely used early 19th century architectural style and source book, for colonial up into Greek Revival periods. Extensive development of geometry of carpentering, construction of sashes, frames, doors, stairs; plans and elevations of domestic and other buildings. Hundreds of thousands of houses were built according to this book, now invaluable to historians, architects, restorers, etc. 1827 edition. 59 plates. 114pp. 7⅞ x 10¾.
22236-5 Paperbound $3.50

Dutch Houses in the Hudson Valley Before 1776, Helen Wilkinson Reynolds. The standard survey of the Dutch colonial house and outbuildings, with constructional features, decoration, and local history associated with individual homesteads. Introduction by Franklin D. Roosevelt. Map. 150 illustrations. 469pp. 6⅝ x 9¼.   21469-9 Paperbound $4.00

POEMS OF ANNE BRADSTREET, edited with an introduction by Robert Hutchinson. A new selection of poems by America's first poet and perhaps the first significant woman poet in the English language. 48 poems display her development in works of considerable variety—love poems, domestic poems, religious meditations, formal elegies, "quaternions," etc. Notes, bibliography. viii + 222pp.

22160-1 Paperbound $2.00

THREE GOTHIC NOVELS: THE CASTLE OF OTRANTO BY HORACE WALPOLE; VATHEK BY WILLIAM BECKFORD; THE VAMPYRE BY JOHN POLIDORI, WITH FRAGMENT OF A NOVEL BY LORD BYRON, edited by E. F. Bleiler. The first Gothic novel, by Walpole; the finest Oriental tale in English, by Beckford; powerful Romantic supernatural story in versions by Polidori and Byron. All extremely important in history of literature; all still exciting, packed with supernatural thrills, ghosts, haunted castles, magic, etc. xl + 291pp.

21232-7 Paperbound $2.00

THE BEST TALES OF HOFFMANN, E. T. A. Hoffmann. 10 of Hoffmann's most important stories, in modern re-editings of standard translations: Nutcracker and the King of Mice, Signor Formica, Automata, The Sandman, Rath Krespel, The Golden Flowerpot, Master Martin the Cooper, The Mines of Falun, The King's Betrothed, A New Year's Eve Adventure. 7 illustrations by Hoffmann. Edited by E. F. Bleiler. xxxix + 419pp.

21793-0 Paperbound $2.50

GHOST AND HORROR STORIES OF AMBROSE BIERCE, Ambrose Bierce. 23 strikingly modern stories of the horrors latent in the human mind: The Eyes of the Panther, The Damned Thing, An Occurrence at Owl Creek Bridge, An Inhabitant of Carcosa, etc., plus the dream-essay, Visions of the Night. Edited by E. F. Bleiler. xxii + 199pp.

20767-6 Paperbound $1.50

BEST GHOST STORIES OF J. S. LEFANU, J. Sheridan LeFanu. Finest stories by Victorian master often considered greatest supernatural writer of all. Carmilla, Green Tea, The Haunted Baronet, The Familiar, and 12 others. Most never before available in the U. S. A. Edited by E. F. Bleiler. 8 illustrations from Victorian publications. xvii + 467pp.

20415-4 Paperbound $2.50

THE TIME STREAM, THE GREATEST ADVENTURE, AND THE PURPLE SAPPHIRE—THREE SCIENCE FICTION NOVELS, John Taine (Eric Temple Bell). Great American mathematician was also foremost science fiction novelist of the 1920's. *The Time Stream,* one of all-time classics, uses concepts of circular time; *The Greatest Adventure,* incredibly ancient biological experiments from Antarctica threaten to escape; The *Purple Sapphire,* superscience, lost races in Central Tibet, survivors of the Great Race. 4 illustrations by Frank R. Paul. v + 532pp.

21180-0 Paperbound $3.00

SEVEN SCIENCE FICTION NOVELS, H. G. Wells. The standard collection of the great novels. Complete, unabridged. *First Men in the Moon, Island of Dr. Moreau, War of the Worlds, Food of the Gods, Invisible Man, Time Machine, In the Days of the Comet.* Not only science fiction fans, but every educated person owes it to himself to read these novels. 1015pp.

20264-X Clothbound $5.00

JOHANN SEBASTIAN BACH, Philipp Spitta. One of the great classics of musicology, this definitive analysis of Bach's music (and life) has never been surpassed. Lucid, nontechnical analyses of hundreds of pieces (30 pages devoted to St. Matthew Passion, 26 to B Minor Mass). Also includes major analysis of 18th-century music. 450 musical examples. 40-page musical supplement. Total of xx + 1799pp.
(EUK) 22278-0, 22279-9 Two volumes, Clothbound $15.00

MOZART AND HIS PIANO CONCERTOS, Cuthbert Girdlestone. The only full-length study of an important area of Mozart's creativity. Provides detailed analyses of all 23 concertos, traces inspirational sources. 417 musical examples. Second edition. 509pp. (USO) 21271-8 Paperbound $3.50

THE PERFECT WAGNERITE: A COMMENTARY ON THE NIBLUNG'S RING, George Bernard Shaw. Brilliant and still relevant criticism in remarkable essays on Wagner's Ring cycle, Shaw's ideas on political and social ideology behind the plots, role of Leitmotifs, vocal requisites, etc. Prefaces. xxi + 136pp.
21707-8 Paperbound $1.50

DON GIOVANNI, W. A. Mozart. Complete libretto, modern English translation; biographies of composer and librettist; accounts of early performances and critical reaction. Lavishly illustrated. All the material you need to understand and appreciate this great work. Dover Opera Guide and Libretto Series; translated and introduced by Ellen Bleiler. 92 illustrations. 209pp.
21134-7 Paperbound $1.50

HIGH FIDELITY SYSTEMS: A LAYMAN'S GUIDE, Roy F. Allison. All the basic information you need for setting up your own audio system: high fidelity and stereo record players, tape records, F.M. Connections, adjusting tone arm, cartridge, checking needle alignment, positioning speakers, phasing speakers, adjusting hums, trouble-shooting, maintenance, and similar topics. Enlarged 1965 edition. More than 50 charts, diagrams, photos. iv + 91pp. 21514-8 Paperbound $1.25

REPRODUCTION OF SOUND, Edgar Villchur. Thorough coverage for laymen of high fidelity systems, reproducing systems in general, needles, amplifiers, preamps, loudspeakers, feedback, explaining physical background. "A rare talent for making technicalities vividly comprehensible," R. Darrell, *High Fidelity*. 69 figures. iv + 92pp. 21515-6 Paperbound $1.25

HEAR ME TALKIN' TO YA: THE STORY OF JAZZ AS TOLD BY THE MEN WHO MADE IT, Nat Shapiro and Nat Hentoff. Louis Armstrong, Fats Waller, Jo Jones, Clarence Williams, Billy Holiday, Duke Ellington, Jelly Roll Morton and dozens of other jazz greats tell how it was in Chicago's South Side, New Orleans, depression Harlem and the modern West Coast as jazz was born and grew. xvi + 429pp.
21726-4 Paperbound $2.50

FABLES OF AESOP, translated by Sir Roger L'Estrange. A reproduction of the very rare 1931 Paris edition; a selection of the most interesting fables, together with 50 imaginative drawings by Alexander Calder. v + 128pp. 6½x9¼.
21780-9 Paperbound $1.50

CATALOGUE OF DOVER BOOKS

THE RED FAIRY BOOK, Andrew Lang. Lang's color fairy books have long been children's favorites. This volume includes Rapunzel, Jack and the Bean-stalk and 35 other stories, familiar and unfamiliar. 4 plates, 93 illustrations x + 367pp.
21673-X Paperbound $2.50

THE BLUE FAIRY BOOK, Andrew Lang. Lang's tales come from all countries and all times. Here are 37 tales from Grimm, the Arabian Nights, Greek Mythology, and other fascinating sources. 8 plates, 130 illustrations. xi + 390pp.
21437-0 Paperbound $2.50

HOUSEHOLD STORIES BY THE BROTHERS GRIMM. Classic English-language edition of the well-known tales — Rumpelstiltskin, Snow White, Hansel and Gretel, The Twelve Brothers, Faithful John, Rapunzel, Tom Thumb (52 stories in all). Translated into simple, straightforward English by Lucy Crane. Ornamented with head-pieces, vignettes, elaborate decorative initials and a dozen full-page illustrations by Walter Crane. x + 269pp.
21080-4 Paperbound $2.50

THE MERRY ADVENTURES OF ROBIN HOOD, Howard Pyle. The finest modern versions of the traditional ballads and tales about the great English outlaw. Howard Pyle's complete prose version, with every word, every illustration of the first edition. Do not confuse this facsimile of the original (1883) with modern editions that change text or illustrations. 23 plates plus many page decorations. xxii + 296pp.
22043-5 Paperbound $2.50

THE STORY OF KING ARTHUR AND HIS KNIGHTS, Howard Pyle. The finest children's version of the life of King Arthur; brilliantly retold by Pyle, with 48 of his most imaginative illustrations. xviii + 313pp. 6⅛ x 9¼.
21445-1 Paperbound $2.50

THE WONDERFUL WIZARD OF OZ, L. Frank Baum. America's finest children's book in facsimile of first edition with all Denslow illustrations in full color. The edition a child should have. Introduction by Martin Gardner. 23 color plates, scores of drawings. iv + 267pp.
20691-2 Paperbound $2.50

THE MARVELOUS LAND OF OZ, L. Frank Baum. The second Oz book, every bit as imaginative as the Wizard. The hero is a boy named Tip, but the Scarecrow and the Tin Woodman are back, as is the Oz magic. 16 color plates, 120 drawings by John R. Neill. 287pp.
20692-0 Paperbound $2.50

THE MAGICAL MONARCH OF MO, L. Frank Baum. Remarkable adventures in a land even stranger than Oz. The best of Baum's books not in the Oz series. 15 color plates and dozens of drawings by Frank Verbeck. xviii + 237pp.
21892-9 Paperbound $2.25

THE BAD CHILD'S BOOK OF BEASTS, MORE BEASTS FOR WORSE CHILDREN, A MORAL ALPHABET, Hilaire Belloc. Three complete humor classics in one volume. Be kind to the frog, and do not call him names . . . and 28 other whimsical animals. Familiar favorites and some not so well known. Illustrated by Basil Blackwell.
156pp.
(USO) 20749-8 Paperbound $1.50

EAST O' THE SUN AND WEST O' THE MOON, George W. Dasent. Considered the best of all translations of these Norwegian folk tales, this collection has been enjoyed by generations of children (and folklorists too). Includes True and Untrue, Why the Sea is Salt, East O' the Sun and West O' the Moon, Why the Bear is Stumpy-Tailed, Boots and the Troll, The Cock and the Hen, Rich Peter the Pedlar, and 52 more. The only edition with all 59 tales. 77 illustrations by Erik Werenskiold and Theodor Kittelsen. xv + 418pp. 22521-6 Paperbound $3.50

GOOPS AND HOW TO BE THEM, Gelett Burgess. Classic of tongue-in-cheek humor, masquerading as etiquette book. 87 verses, twice as many cartoons, show mischievous Goops as they demonstrate to children virtues of table manners, neatness, courtesy, etc. Favorite for generations. viii + 88pp. $6\frac{1}{2}$ x $9\frac{1}{4}$.
22233-0 Paperbound $1.25

ALICE'S ADVENTURES UNDER GROUND, Lewis Carroll. The first version, quite different from the final Alice in Wonderland, printed out by Carroll himself with his own illustrations. Complete facsimile of the "million dollar" manuscript Carroll gave to Alice Liddell in 1864. Introduction by Martin Gardner. viii + 96pp. Title and dedication pages in color. 21482-6 Paperbound $1.25

THE BROWNIES, THEIR BOOK, Palmer Cox. Small as mice, cunning as foxes, exuberant and full of mischief, the Brownies go to the zoo, toy shop, seashore, circus, etc., in 24 verse adventures and 266 illustrations. Long a favorite, since their first appearance in St. Nicholas Magazine. xi + 144pp. $6\frac{5}{8}$ x $9\frac{1}{4}$.
21265-3 Paperbound $1.75

SONGS OF CHILDHOOD, Walter De La Mare. Published (under the pseudonym Walter Ramal) when De La Mare was only 29, this charming collection has long been a favorite children's book. A facsimile of the first edition in paper, the 47 poems capture the simplicity of the nursery rhyme and the ballad, including such lyrics as I Met Eve, Tartary, The Silver Penny. vii + 106pp. 21972-0 Paperbound $1.25

THE COMPLETE NONSENSE OF EDWARD LEAR, Edward Lear. The finest 19th-century humorist-cartoonist in full: all nonsense limericks, zany alphabets, Owl and Pussycat, songs, nonsense botany, and more than 500 illustrations by Lear himself. Edited by Holbrook Jackson. xxix + 287pp. (USO) 20167-8 Paperbound $2.00

BILLY WHISKERS: THE AUTOBIOGRAPHY OF A GOAT, Frances Trego Montgomery. A favorite of children since the early 20th century, here are the escapades of that rambunctious, irresistible and mischievous goat—Billy Whiskers. Much in the spirit of Peck's Bad Boy, this is a book that children never tire of reading or hearing. All the original familiar illustrations by W. H. Fry are included: 6 color plates, 18 black and white drawings. 159pp. 22345-0 Paperbound $2.00

MOTHER GOOSE MELODIES. Faithful republication of the fabulously rare Munroe and Francis "copyright 1833" Boston edition—the most important Mother Goose collection, usually referred to as the "original." Familiar rhymes plus many rare ones, with wonderful old woodcut illustrations. Edited by E. F. Bleiler. 128pp. $4\frac{1}{2}$ x $6\frac{3}{8}$. 22577-1 Paperbound $1.25

Two Little Savages; Being the Adventures of Two Boys Who Lived as Indians and What They Learned, Ernest Thompson Seton. Great classic of nature and boyhood provides a vast range of woodlore in most palatable form, a genuinely entertaining story. Two farm boys build a teepee in woods and live in it for a month, working out Indian solutions to living problems, star lore, birds and animals, plants, etc. 293 illustrations. vii + 286pp.

20985-7 Paperbound $2.50

Peter Piper's Practical Principles of Plain & Perfect Pronunciation. Alliterative jingles and tongue-twisters of surprising charm, that made their first appearance in America about 1830. Republished in full with the spirited woodcut illustrations from this earliest American edition. 32pp. 4½ x 6⅜.

22560-7 Paperbound $1.00

Science Experiments and Amusements for Children, Charles Vivian. 73 easy experiments, requiring only materials found at home or easily available, such as candles, coins, steel wool, etc.; illustrate basic phenomena like vacuum, simple chemical reaction, etc. All safe. Modern, well-planned. Formerly *Science Games for Children*. 102 photos, numerous drawings. 96pp. 6⅛ x 9¼.

21856-2 Paperbound $1.25

An Introduction to Chess Moves and Tactics Simply Explained, Leonard Barden. Informal intermediate introduction, quite strong in explaining reasons for moves. Covers basic material, tactics, important openings, traps, positional play in middle game, end game. Attempts to isolate patterns and recurrent configurations. Formerly *Chess*. 58 figures. 102pp. (USO) 21210-6 Paperbound $1.25

Lasker's Manual of Chess, Dr. Emanuel Lasker. Lasker was not only one of the five great World Champions, he was also one of the ablest expositors, theorists, and analysts. In many ways, his Manual, permeated with his philosophy of battle, filled with keen insights, is one of the greatest works ever written on chess. Filled with analyzed games by the great players. A single-volume library that will profit almost any chess player, beginner or master. 308 diagrams. xli x 349pp.

20640-8 Paperbound $2.75

The Master Book of Mathematical Recreations, Fred Schuh. In opinion of many the finest work ever prepared on mathematical puzzles, stunts, recreations; exhaustively thorough explanations of mathematics involved, analysis of effects, citation of puzzles and games. Mathematics involved is elementary. Translated by F. Göbel. 194 figures. xxiv + 430pp. 22134-2 Paperbound $3.00

Mathematics, Magic and Mystery, Martin Gardner. Puzzle editor for Scientific American explains mathematics behind various mystifying tricks: card tricks, stage "mind reading," coin and match tricks, counting out games, geometric dissections, etc. Probability sets, theory of numbers clearly explained. Also provides more than 400 tricks, guaranteed to work, that you can do. 135 illustrations. xii + 176pp.

20338-2 Paperbound $1.50

"ESSENTIAL GRAMMAR" SERIES

All you really need to know about modern, colloquial grammar. Many educational shortcuts help you learn faster, understand better. Detailed cognate lists teach you to recognize similarities between English and foreign words and roots—make learning vocabulary easy and interesting. Excellent for independent study or as a supplement to record courses.

ESSENTIAL FRENCH GRAMMAR, Seymour Resnick. 2500-item cognate list. 159pp.
(EBE) 20419-7 Paperbound $1.25

ESSENTIAL GERMAN GRAMMAR, Guy Stern and Everett F. Bleiler. Unusual shortcuts on noun declension, word order, compound verbs. 124pp.
(EBE) 20422-7 Paperbound $1.25

ESSENTIAL ITALIAN GRAMMAR, Olga Ragusa. 111pp.
(EBE) 20779-X Paperbound $1.25

ESSENTIAL JAPANESE GRAMMAR, Everett F. Bleiler. In Romaji transcription; no characters needed. Japanese grammar is regular and simple. 156pp.
21027-8 Paperbound $1.25

ESSENTIAL PORTUGUESE GRAMMAR, Alexander da R. Prista. vi + 114pp.
21650-0 Paperbound $1.35

ESSENTIAL SPANISH GRAMMAR, Seymour Resnick. 2500 word cognate list. 115pp.
(EBE) 20780-3 Paperbound $1.25

ESSENTIAL ENGLISH GRAMMAR, Philip Gucker. Combines best features of modern, functional and traditional approaches. For refresher, class use, home study. x + 177pp.
21649-7 Paperbound $1.35

A PHRASE AND SENTENCE DICTIONARY OF SPOKEN SPANISH. Prepared for U. S. War Department by U. S. linguists. As above, unit is idiom, phrase or sentence rather than word. English-Spanish and Spanish-English sections contain modern equivalents of over 18,000 sentences. Introduction and appendix as above. iv + 513pp.
20495-2 Paperbound $2.75

A PHRASE AND SENTENCE DICTIONARY OF SPOKEN RUSSIAN. Dictionary prepared for U. S. War Department by U. S. linguists. Basic unit is not the word, but the idiom, phrase or sentence. English-Russian and Russian-English sections contain modern equivalents for over 30,000 phrases. Grammatical introduction covers phonetics, writing, syntax. Appendix of word lists for food, numbers, geographical names, etc. vi + 573 pp. 6⅛ x 9¼.
20496-0 Paperbound $4.00

CONVERSATIONAL CHINESE FOR BEGINNERS, Morris Swadesh. Phonetic system, beginner's course in Pai Hua Mandarin Chinese covering most important, most useful speech patterns. Emphasis on modern colloquial usage. Formerly *Chinese in Your Pocket.* xvi + 158pp.
21123-1 Paperbound $1.75

MATHEMATICAL PUZZLES FOR BEGINNERS AND ENTHUSIASTS, Geoffrey Mott-Smith. 189 puzzles from easy to difficult—involving arithmetic, logic, algebra, properties of digits, probability, etc.—for enjoyment and mental stimulus. Explanation of mathematical principles behind the puzzles. 135 illustrations. viii + 248pp.
20198-8 Paperbound $1.75

PAPER FOLDING FOR BEGINNERS, William D. Murray and Francis J. Rigney. Easiest book on the market, clearest instructions on making interesting, beautiful origami. Sail boats, cups, roosters, frogs that move legs, bonbon boxes, standing birds, etc. 40 projects; more than 275 diagrams and photographs. 94pp.
20713-7 Paperbound $1.00

TRICKS AND GAMES ON THE POOL TABLE, Fred Herrmann. 79 tricks and games— some solitaires, some for two or more players, some competitive games—to entertain you between formal games. Mystifying shots and throws, unusual caroms, tricks involving such props as cork, coins, a hat, etc. Formerly *Fun on the Pool Table.* 77 figures. 95pp.
21814-7 Paperbound $1.00

HAND SHADOWS TO BE THROWN UPON THE WALL: A SERIES OF NOVEL AND AMUSING FIGURES FORMED BY THE HAND, Henry Bursill. Delightful picturebook from great-grandfather's day shows how to make 18 different hand shadows: a bird that flies, duck that quacks, dog that wags his tail, camel, goose, deer, boy, turtle, etc. Only book of its sort. vi + 33pp. 6½ x 9¼. 21779-5 Paperbound $1.00

WHITTLING AND WOODCARVING, E. J. Tangerman. 18th printing of best book on market. "If you can cut a potato you can carve" toys and puzzles, chains, chessmen, caricatures, masks, frames, woodcut blocks, surface patterns, much more. Information on tools, woods, techniques. Also goes into serious wood sculpture from Middle Ages to present, East and West. 464 photos, figures. x + 293pp.
20965-2 Paperbound $2.00

HISTORY OF PHILOSOPHY, Julián Marias. Possibly the clearest, most easily followed, best planned, most useful one-volume history of philosophy on the market; neither skimpy nor overfull. Full details on system of every major philosopher and dozens of less important thinkers from pre-Socratics up to Existentialism and later. Strong on many European figures usually omitted. Has gone through dozens of editions in Europe. 1966 edition, translated by Stanley Appelbaum and Clarence Strowbridge. xviii + 505pp. 21739-6 Paperbound $3.00

YOGA: A SCIENTIFIC EVALUATION, Kovoor T. Behanan. Scientific but non-technical study of physiological results of yoga exercises; done under auspices of Yale U. Relations to Indian thought, to psychoanalysis, etc. 16 photos. xxiii + 270pp.
20505-3 Paperbound $2.50

Prices subject to change without notice.
Available at your book dealer or write for free catalogue to Dept. GI, Dover Publications, Inc., 180 Varick St., N. Y., N. Y. 10014. Dover publishes more than 150 books each year on science, elementary and advanced mathematics, biology, music, art, literary history, social sciences and other areas.